Politics, Gangs, and Vodou

Politics, Gangs, and Vodou

Haiti's Struggle for Democracy
and Human Rights

YVON MILIEN

Politics, Gangs, and Vodou: Haiti's Struggle for Democracy and Human Rights

Politics, Sociology, Anthropology, Philosophy

Copyright © 2025 by Yvon Milien

Address all inquiries to: ymilien@hotmail.com

Because of the dynamic nature of the internet, any web addresses or links contained in this book may have changed since publication and may no longer be valid.

ISBN: 979-8-9860364-4-1 (print)
ISBN: 979-8-9860364-5-8 (e-book)

Library of Congress Control Number: 2025915146

Back cover photography by John Ricard.

Printed by IngramSpark in the United States of America.

Published by Yvon Milien.

Visit www.yvonmilien.com

To the resilient Haitian people.

To those who rise before dawn, walking barefoot on broken roads, courageously planting seeds of hope in soil soaked with tears.

This book is dedicated to you: the children who dare to dream by candlelight, and the elders who hold the memories of a freer Haiti.

To those who have succumbed to despair, who no longer believe that justice, like the sun, will inevitably rise with the morning.

And to all who remain steadfast in the conviction that justice, like the sun, can shine once more over this beautiful yet burdened land.

Haiti's voice is stronger when we choose to speak;

it is weaker when we encourage violence.

CONTENTS

Haiti, History, and Hope

When memory fails, and awareness sleeps,
democracy decays into a land of the living dead—
where hollow leaders rise and lead the blind.

—Epigraph by the author

Paraphrasing the French philosopher Emmanuel Mounier, one might say that the story of any people is the story of their sense of inadequacy—and their stubborn, sometimes heroic efforts to rise above it. This insight has lingered in my heart for years, but it strikes especially close to home when I reflect on Haiti: its people, its past, its pain, and its persistent hope.

Why do some nations struggle so long to shake off the weight of history and injustice? Why do others rise while some—like Haiti—seem always on the edge of promise, yet are always held back by crisis? These questions have shaped my life and guided my writing. I first felt them deeply as a young man on a bright November morning in 1987, the day Haitians were to participate in our first free democratic elections in decades. I was dressed in my Sunday best, my voter card clutched in hand, my heart full of hope. But by midmorning, that hope was shattered. What should have been a celebration of liberty turned into the Ruelle Vaillant massacre—an eruption of violence that left bodies in the street where ballots should have been cast.

That day has never left me. I've asked myself ever since: *Why must people be gunned down for daring to dream of dignity? Why must democracy cost so much blood?*

This book is my attempt to answer those questions—not just with facts and history, but with feeling and honesty. It is written from a place of deep love for Haiti and a longing to see her people flourish—not as beggars at the table of foreign aid but as proud architects of their own destiny. This is not a book of pity. It is a book of purpose.

Though the topics it explores—politics, gangs, vodou, democracy, human rights—may seem heavy, they are not distant. They shape real lives. They govern how people live, suffer, and dream. And they are not unique to Haiti. Anyone who cares about justice, the dignity of human life, and the hard path to freedom will find something familiar here. This is not just Haiti's story—it is a human story.

Understanding Haiti's present condition requires that we look back—sometimes painfully—at the past. Several historical events continue to cast long shadows: the brutal colonial system of Saint-Domingue, which fueled France's wealth and left behind a legacy of trauma and inequality; the 1804 revolution, which created the world's first Black republic but also provoked isolation and punishment from the global powers of the time; the US occupation from 1915 to 1934, which restructured Haitian institutions to serve foreign interests and left behind a militarized legacy; the Duvalier dictatorship, which reigned through fear, paramilitarism, and the systematic dismantling of civic life; and the repeated cycles of coups, foreign interventions, and fragile democratic experiments that followed. These events did not simply occur and then disappear. They engraved themselves into the nation's institutions, its memory, and its soul.

But if history has helped build the walls of Haiti's current prison, then knowledge of that same history can show us the way out. To know the story in full is to see where the cracks in the foundation lie—and how they might be repaired. It is to reclaim agency, restore dignity, and imagine a future not dictated by the past but informed by its hard-earned wisdom.

You don't have to be Haitian to care. You don't need a passport or a PhD. What Haiti needs most is not just money but understanding. Not charity but solidarity. Not pity but partnership. Global citizens can support Haiti in powerful ways beyond traditional foreign aid—by advocating for just international policies, supporting Haitian-led initiatives, amplifying Haitian voices, holding governments accountable for exploitative practices, and—perhaps most important—by learning and teaching the truth about Haiti's history. Empathy is not a substitute for action, but it is the soil in which meaningful, lasting change can grow.

The seed of this book was planted long ago, during my days as a student of communication. It was then, as I wrestled with the tragedy of Haiti's illiteracy, that the vision of this work first stirred within me. What began as a student's reflection has grown, over years of experience and contemplation, into the book you now hold. At that time, I believed—and still believe—that a nation that cannot read cannot be free. Yet I have since come to understand that literacy goes beyond reading letters on a page: it is the ability to read history, to read the times we live in, and to discern truth from falsehood.

And so, the idea of this book grew—broader, deeper, and more relentless, yet still burning with the same original conviction. Haiti's pain is no accident; it is the bitter harvest of centuries of domination, corruption, neglect, and betrayal—many of them perpetuated by those who claimed to lead. But history is not a prison. If we dare to understand how we arrived here—if we refuse to look away—then we can change our destiny. We can strike a new note, and together, we can rewrite our nation's song.

This book is not a lament. It's a confrontation—and an invitation. It confronts the political machinery that smothers hope. It confronts the way gangs rise in the cracks of failed justice. It confronts how vodou is misused and misunderstood. It confronts the silence that lets the worst things thrive.

But it also invites you to look deeper. To see the strength that still exists. The culture that still sings. The people who still resist. It dares to imagine a Haiti beyond dependency and despair—a Haiti of justice, resilience, and light.

This book serves as a compass for the Haitian soul—a guide for aspiring leaders, civic-minded citizens, journalists, educators, and members of the international community who seek to walk alongside Haiti, not ahead of her, in the long march toward democracy and human dignity.

It primarily speaks to the youth, to conscious leaders emerging from the ashes of disillusionment, and to institutions—notably, the Haitian media and international actors—who are ready to exchange symbolic gestures for genuine, sustained commitment.

More than a chronicle of political turmoil, *Politics, Gangs, and Vodou* is a map and a mirror. It offers a blueprint for both the ordinary and the well-informed Haitian citizen to grasp the essence of democracy: not merely as a system of elections or slogans, but as a living, breathing culture of participation, justice, and accountability. It invites readers to examine the fragile social contract and ask difficult, often painful, questions: Who truly governs? What invisible hands shape public life? And what happens when the people mistake tyranny for strength or institutions trade public service for private gain?

This book also aims to awaken the public to the signs of manipulation and danger—to recognize when they are trapped in a toxic entanglement with false leaders, criminal networks, or foreign interests masquerading as saviors. It requires discernment, vigilance, and above all, moral courage.

In these pages, readers will find not only analysis and testimony but also a moral appeal—a call to reclaim Haiti's promise through democratic renewal, cultural pride, and spiritual integrity. Haiti's future will not be decided solely in foreign embassies or presidential palaces, but in the conscience of its people.

Politics, Gangs, and Vodou is not an academic monograph, a compilation of scholarly essays, or a traditional historical textbook. Instead, it is a work of nonfiction crafted for the general reader—an invitation to explore and understand the complex and often misunderstood reality of Haiti. Written in an accessible yet thoughtful style, the book seeks to illuminate the nation's political struggles, cultural resilience, spiritual heritage, and the enduring challenges it faces, offering insight without jargon and narrative without pretense.

How to Read This Book

The chapters are structured to help readers journey through Haiti's past and present, understanding not only *what happened* but *why it matters*. You'll find a mix of historical narrative, personal reflection, and careful analysis. This is a book meant to be read with both the mind and the heart.

If you're reading to understand the whole picture, I recommend starting from the beginning and following each part in sequence. Each part builds on the previous one. But if you're drawn to a particular subject—say, human rights, the role of gangs, or the history of vodou—you're welcome to begin there and reevaluate as needed. The book is designed to be both a continuous journey and a resource to return to again and again.

Here's how it unfolds:

- **Part I** describes the country, its people, and where they come from, as well as their culture, societal norms, religions, and so on.
- **Part II** sets the stage with a historical, social, and political overview of Haiti—from independence to the brink of restored democracy.
- **Part III** defines key concepts, such as authoritarianism, democracy, and human rights, providing a practical framework for understanding the material that follows.
- **Part IV** compares life under a dictatorship and democratic rule, measuring how far (or how little) rights and freedoms have progressed.

- **Part V** zooms in on the before and after, highlighting the sharpest differences in how people have lived, suffered, and hoped.

- **Part VI** ties these threads together, reflecting on what Haiti's past reveals about its present—and its future.

- **Part VII** tackles the rise of gangs and their entanglement with vodou, politics, and daily survival.

- **Part VIII** returns to the roots, exploring Haiti's colonial history and the long shadow of empire that still shapes its institutions and identity.

- **Part IX** examines how militarization—from independence through the Duvalier years and beyond—has warped the idea of governance and democracy.

- **Part X** turns to the bright flame of resistance, tracing Haiti's long tradition of protest, faith-based activism, and grassroots courage.

- **Part XI** reveals how democratic ideals have been betrayed—through division, corruption, foreign interference, and the erosion of sovereignty.

- **Part XII** looks forward, imagining a new vision of Haitian democracy—one built on dignity, justice, civic strength, and a renewed national identity. It calls on the media and all of us to play our part in writing a new covenant for the future.

This book is not just about understanding what has gone wrong. It's about what *can* go right—if we choose differently. If we listen. If we learn. If we act with courage.

So I invite you to step into this story. Walk with Haiti through its long night and dare to imagine the dawn. Let your mind be sharpened and your heart stirred. And if, in the end, you see Haiti not with pity but with kinship, not as a problem to be solved but as a people to be respected—then this book will have done its work.

Let us begin.

PART I

Haiti and the Soul of Its People

CHAPTER 1

A People Forged in Fire:
Haiti's Land, Culture, and Legacy

Fire tempers a nation's identity like steel—its trials give it strength,
its struggles shape its form, and memory cools it into soul.

—Epigraph by the author

What do you genuinely know about Haiti? Beyond the headlines of disaster or political unrest, have you ever asked: Who are the Haitian people? What shaped their spirit, their culture, their faith, and their way of life? What historical forces forged a society so deeply wounded yet so enduringly proud?

To understand Haiti's present political struggles, we must first comprehend the people and the cultural context from which those struggles emerge.

This section invites you to look past the surface and step into the soul of Haiti—to meet a people forged in fire whose legacy cannot be separated from their land, their memory, and their ongoing resistance to despair. From the Indigenous Taíno who once called this land home to the descendants of African slaves who shaped its soul, Haiti's story is unlike any other.

The Land Before Haiti

Long before the world knew the name *Haiti*, the land was home to the Taíno, a branch of the Arawak people who had migrated north from South America. They called the island *Ayiti*—meaning *land of high mountains*—a name still spoken with reverence today. The Taíno lived in organized communities, practiced agriculture, wove baskets, carved ceremonial objects, and held elaborate religious rituals centered on *zemis*, or ancestral spirits. Their society, while not without hierarchy, was communal, spiritual, and remarkably in tune with the natural world.

Then came the Spanish, with their swords and smallpox, and the balance was shattered. Within a few short decades, the Taíno population was virtually wiped out through forced labor, disease, and outright slaughter. The soul of *Ayiti* was scarred but not silenced.

From Bondage to Birth

Following the decimation of the Indigenous population, the Spanish and later the French turned to West Africa for forced labor. Over the course of the seventeenth and eighteenth centuries, hundreds of thousands of Africans were brought to the colony of Saint-Domingue—the western third of the island—under one of the most brutal plantation regimes in the history of the Americas. These men and women, torn from the shores of Dahomey, Kongo, Senegal, Yoruba, and beyond, carried with them languages, religions, memories, rhythms, and philosophies. These would become the spiritual bedrock of Haitian identity.

The Roots of a Plantation Empire: How It All Began

How did a small Caribbean island become the wealthiest colony in the world?

How did the soil of Saint-Domingue—today's Haiti—come to enrich France with unimaginable wealth while enslaving hundreds of thousands of human beings in the process?

And how did the very system that made Saint-Domingue a jewel of the French empire also plant the seeds of its destruction?

To understand the origins of Haiti's struggle, we must begin with this stark truth: The island was once the engine of French colonial prosperity, built on some of the most fertile land in the Western Hemisphere and sustained by the relentless labor of enslaved Africans.

From the early 1700s until the eve of the Haitian Revolution in the 1790s, Saint-Domingue flourished as the crown jewel of France's overseas empire. The land was stunningly rich: lush valleys, rain-fed hillsides, and volcanic soil made even the mountaintops productive. Nowhere in Europe could one imagine such fecundity. Yet this natural abundance was not enough. To turn soil into profit, France imported Africans by the hundreds of thousands, forcing them to labor in sugar and coffee plantations under brutal, dehumanizing conditions.

By the late eighteenth century, more than four hundred and fifty thousand enslaved Africans toiled in Saint-Domingue—a population nearly ten times greater than that of the White colonists. And yet, this highly unequal and fragile society managed to produce staggering wealth. Dalmas, drawing on official French colonial statistics, reports that sugar and coffee exports alone generated as much as 400 million francs annually. These profits fed France's economy, built its cities, enriched its merchants, and filled the royal treasury. The island was responsible for two-thirds of France's entire colonial trade—a figure that reveals just how dependent the empire had become on the backs of the enslaved.

To manage this colonial machine, France established a strict system of governance: a governor-general, an intendant, local councils, and a web of laws to ensure order, maximize output, and secure French interests. More than twenty towns were built to support trade, and every aspect of life in Saint-Domingue revolved around plantation agriculture, slavery, and profit.

Sugar and coffee were not just commodities—they were the lifeblood of the colony. And slavery was not merely tolerated: it was the very foundation of this colonial order. Without enslaved labor, there would have been no sugar empire. Without those crops, there would have been no justification, at least economically, for slavery in Saint-Domingue. The two systems were intertwined—feeding each other, sustaining each other—until the system collapsed under the weight of its violence and contradiction.

A Paradise Built on Chains

The story of Saint-Domingue is not merely a tale of riches and industry—it is also a story of tragedy, injustice, and moral blindness. For more than a century, the island stood as a testament to what the colonial world could extract when nature's bounty was combined with human exploitation. But it also stood, unknowingly, on the edge of a storm. The very wealth that Saint-Domingue generated for France came at the cost of deep social divisions, immense human suffering, and a volatile imbalance of power.

Even before the Haitian Revolution, some French voices saw the reckoning coming. As Abbé Raynal, the fiery French Enlightenment thinker and fierce critic of colonial slavery, warned in 1770, long before the uprising began: "The master's security lies in the slave's ignorance; but when this fragile illusion disappears, when the slave understands the weight of his chains, nothing can hold back the force of nature claiming its rights."[1]

The seeds of resistance were already taking root. The land that once produced gold for Europe would soon give birth to the world's first Black republic—a revolution forged in fire, blood, and unyielding cries for freedom.

This is how it began. This is what Haiti inherited.

So Saint-Domingue grew wealthy beyond imagination for the French empire, exporting sugar, coffee, and indigo, but at a human cost so monstrous, it ignited rebellion. In 1791, the enslaved rose. And in 1804, after more than a decade of armed resistance and the defeat of Napoleon Bonaparte's troops, Haiti became the first Black republic in the world— and the only nation born of a successful slave revolt.

But independence came with a terrible price. Ostracized by Western powers, forced to pay crippling reparations to France, and burdened by internal divisions, Haiti began its journey as a free nation amid isolation, sabotage, and inherited trauma.

---

[1] This saying, often linked to Abbé Raynal—"The master's security lies in the slave's ignorance..."— does not appear verbatim in his writings. We best understand it as a paraphrase of Raynal's strong condemnation of slavery in the *Histoire philosophique et politique des deux Indes* (1770).

The Haitian People

Haitians are the descendants of survivors—of genocide, slavery, revolution, and foreign occupation. That legacy gives the Haitian character a unique blend of fierce dignity, spiritual depth, humor, hospitality, and resilience. There is a sacred rhythm to Haitian life—a poetry that lives in conversation, music, and movement.

The people are predominantly of African descent, though centuries of migration, intermarriage, and social upheaval have created a complex mix of African, European, Arab, and Indigenous heritage. In Haitian society, class and color still serve as enduring markers, shaped more by history than by biology. The old colonial divisions between the light-skinned *mulâtre* elite and the darker-skinned *noir* majority still echo in politics, education, and opportunity, but those boundaries are no longer absolute.

Language and Identity

Haiti is a bilingual nation. French is the language of law, government, and education—an inheritance from colonial rule. But Haitian Creole (*Kreyòl Ayisyen*), born from the blending of African languages with French and shaped by oral tradition, is the heartbeat of the people. It is the language of the home, the market, the prayer circle, and the protest chant. To speak Creole is to be connected to Haiti's soul.

Religion and Spirituality

Haiti is, above all, a profoundly spiritual nation. Roman Catholicism is the dominant religion, followed by Protestantism; however, these two alone do not capture the entire picture. Vodou—rooted in African cosmology and adapted under Catholic imagery—is considered by some to be a religion and by others to be a form of collective psychotherapy, a worldview, a living system of ethics, medicine, a community, and a relationship with the divine. It is not devil worship, as it is often misrepresented. It is an ancestral memory in motion. Some use it negatively while others use it positively. It is the nature of some humans to turn things upside down, especially where laws and morals are not strongly present.

Religious life in Haiti is rarely rigid. Many Haitians move among Catholicism, Protestantism, and vodou without contradiction. The spiritual realm is close: Saints and spirits walk beside the living, and prayer is both a cry for help and a call to resistance.

Education and Literacy

Education in Haiti has long been a battleground. The public system is underfunded and inconsistent; private schools proliferate but often remain inaccessible to the poor. Literacy rates have improved in recent decades, but functional illiteracy, especially in rural areas, remains a challenge. Language plays a role here: Though most Haitians speak Creole, schools often teach in French, alienating children from their linguistic roots.

Despite this, Haiti has produced brilliant writers, philosophers, journalists, and artists who stand tall on the world stage. The Haitian intellectual tradition, rich in resistance and moral clarity, remains one of the nation's proudest legacies.

Culture, Art, and Expression

Haitian culture is a vibrant tapestry. The drumbeat of vodou, the protest songs of the *mizik rasin* movement, the lyricism of poets like René

Depestre and Jacques Roumain, the bold strokes of painters from Jacmel and Cap-Haïtien—these are not luxuries. They are necessities. Art in Haiti is not a refuge from suffering; it is a weapon against it. It tells stories when the newspapers fall silent.

Dance, painting, sculpture, street theater, and even Carnival itself are forms of resistance and joy in the face of adversity. The people express what cannot always be spoken—and preserve what history tried to erase.

Food, Dress, and Daily Life

The Haitian diet reflects both necessity and creativity, featuring staples such as rice and red beans (*diri ak pwa*), fried plantains, spiced meats, *griot*, *soup joumou* (the symbolic New Year's dish of liberty), and fresh tropical fruits. Food is central to the community—families gather not just to eat but to commune.

Traditional dress blends African flair with colonial formality. On market days and festivals, color explodes in handsewn fabrics, beaded sashes, and wide-brimmed hats. Even in poverty, Haitians dress with a sense of dignity and presentation. Appearances matter—not as vanity, but as a statement: *I am here. I matter.*

Most Haitians live in modest housing, often constructed by themselves. In cities, tin roofs and concrete blocks define neighborhoods. In rural areas, clay and wood are the predominant materials. Infrastructure is often fragile, but the spirit of making do—*degaje*—remains a way of life.

The Economy and Work

Haiti's economy is informal, resilient, and often unjust. Agriculture remains the largest source of employment, though the land is overworked and under-supported. Remittances from the diaspora are vital. Many survive through small trade, day labor, and informal markets. Formal employment is scarce. Corruption and dependency have long stifled actual economic development, but local ingenuity persists, from artisans to small-scale manufacturers.

The financial system is a reflection of Haiti's broader inequality: A few hold a significant amount while many have very little. Yet even here, solidarity networks and mutual aid offer glimpses of alternative economic models rooted in community care.

A Nation of Memory and Meaning

Haiti is a country of contradictions: beauty and burden, joy and injustice, history and hope. To understand its current challenges, one must appreciate the people's deep cultural roots and the historical trauma that shaped them. This is not a nation easily explained by statistics or political headlines. It is a nation of memory and meaning, of rhythm and resistance.

The Haitian people carry within them the living legacy of ancestors who endured and overcame. Their story is not finished. By understanding who Haitians are—not just where they are—we move one step closer to a future marked not by pity or intervention but by dignity, solidarity, and respect.

PART II

The Roots of Ruin and Resilience: Haiti's Historical, Social, and Political Foundations

CHAPTER 2

Historical Foundations:
From Chains to Coups:
The Struggle for Sovereignty in Haiti

*The revolution ended the slavery of the body, but the world has never
ceased waging war against the freedom of the soul.*

—Epigraph by the author

W hat happens to a nation born in chains, baptized in fire, and cast
into the world alone?

Can a people who defeated the armies of Europe ever truly be free if the
world refuses to acknowledge their victory? What becomes of liberty when
the soil beneath it is soaked with the blood of betrayal, occupation, and fear?

These are not just historical curiosities—they are living questions in
Haiti, a nation whose past refuses to stay quiet. From the sugarcane fields
of Saint-Domingue to the crowded streets of Port-au-Prince, Haiti's story
is shaped by its bold defiance and the long shadows cast by its colonizers,
its dictators, and at times, even its liberators.

This chapter is a journey through that story: from the extraordinary revolution that gave birth to the first Black republic in 1804 to the return of democratic governance in 1994 and beyond. It is a story of power and loss, of betrayal and survival, of faith and fire. And most of all, it is the story of the Haitian people, who continue to ask—sometimes in anguish, sometimes in hope—"When will our freedom be fulfilled?"

Haiti's story isn't just about battles and borders—it's about people. It's about a nation forged in struggle, tested by betrayal, and still struggling to realize the promise of freedom it once so boldly claimed. To understand Haiti's modern troubles, we must look back, not just to learn about what happened but to grasp why things are the way they are now.

This chapter explores how Haiti evolved politically and socially from the moment it won independence in 1804 to the moment democracy was restored, at least in form, in 1994. It's a journey through revolutions and occupations, dictatorships and dreams. It's also the story of Haitians who refused to give up, even when the odds were impossibly high.

A Nation Born from Slavery and Revolution

When Christopher Columbus arrived in 1492, the island he named *Hispaniola* was already home to the Arawak and Taíno peoples. Within a few generations, these Indigenous groups were nearly wiped out by forced labor, disease, and violence. Later, in the seventeenth century, the western part of the island came under French rule and was renamed Saint-Domingue. It became one of the wealthiest colonies in the world on the backs of hundreds of thousands of enslaved Africans.

By the late eighteenth century, Saint-Domingue had become, as historian C. L. R. James called it, "the richest and most oppressive slave colony the world had ever known." But it was also a powder keg. In 1791, enslaved Africans rose in what would become the only successful slave revolution in world history. Led by extraordinary figures such as Toussaint Louverture, Jean-Jacques Dessalines, and Henri Christophe, the revolutionaries fought against French, British, and Spanish forces— and won.

On January 1, 1804, Dessalines declared the birth of Haiti, the world's first Black republic and the first independent nation in Latin America. But victory came at a heavy price. France demanded a massive indemnity—150 million francs—in exchange for diplomatic recognition. Haiti, under threat of invasion, agreed. Paying that debt crippled its economy for more than a century.

The Wounds of Independence

Though Haiti was free, it was isolated and impoverished. The plantation system had been destroyed, and the international community, led by slaveholding powers like the United States, shunned the new Black republic. Without institutions to support self-rule, Haiti's leaders often relied on force rather than law.

From the start, leadership was fractured. Dessalines was assassinated in 1806. According to Thomas Madiou, the pioneering 19th-century Haitian historian and author of *Histoire d'Haïti*, Dessalines' assassination was the result of a convergence of political rivalries, elite discontent, and fear of despotism. His increasingly authoritarian rule, crowned by his self-proclamation as Emperor, alienated many of his own generals and mulatto elites, who felt excluded from power and threatened by his concentration of authority. His land redistribution policies and militarized agricultural system angered property holders and reminded many of the plantation regime they had just overthrown. Ambitious officers like Pétion, Christophe, Boyer, and others saw him as a tyrant whose harsh methods endangered the young nation's liberty, so they rallied under the banner of "resistance to oppression." Together, these tensions culminated in a conspiracy that lured Dessalines into an ambush at Pont-Rouge, where he was killed—an act Madiou frames as both a revolt against perceived tyranny and the tragic loss of the founding father of Haitian independence. After the tragedy, the country split into rival states—one ruled by Christophe in the north; the other by Alexandre Pétion in the south. While Christophe imposed a harsh regime modeled on plantation discipline, Pétion distributed land to soldiers and peasants, laying the groundwork for Haiti's long tradition of small-scale subsistence farming.

Foreign Interference and Domestic Turmoil

Haiti's internal divisions made it vulnerable to foreign powers. In 1915, US Marines invaded the island after decades of instability and repeated foreign debt crises. The occupation lasted until 1934. The Americans rewrote the constitution, allowing foreigners to own land, and built roads and schools. They also brutalized dissenters and centralized power in the military.

That military structure would later become a tool of dictatorship. In 1957, François "Papa Doc" Duvalier rose to power. A physician by training, Duvalier blended Black Nationalist rhetoric with a ruthless police state. His feared secret police, the Tonton Macoute, terrorized the population. After he died in 1971, his son, Jean-Claude "Baby Doc" Duvalier, took over and continued the repression. Under the Duvaliers, thousands were killed or disappeared, and billions were stolen from the national treasury.

Despite the fear, the opposition never entirely vanished. In the 1980s, protests erupted. In 1986, Jean-Claude was finally ousted. A window for democracy seemed to open—but chaos soon returned.

From Dictatorship to the Edge of Democracy: The 1987 Election That Never Was

After the fall of Jean-Claude in 1986, Haiti entered a period of hope mixed with high anxiety. A military junta, led first by General Henri Namphy, promised to oversee a democratic transition. For the first time in decades, ordinary Haitians dared to believe in the possibility of change through the ballot box rather than through violence or bloodshed.

The political field quickly filled with new and returning voices. Among the most prominent candidates were:

- Marc Louis Bazin, former minister of finance and economy, an economist who once worked at the World Bank. Backed by Haiti's business elite and favored by international powers, he offered a vision of economic reform, stability, and technocratic leadership.
- Gérard Gourgue, former member of the Haitian National Council of Government, the transitional government after the fall of Jean-Claude, from February 1986 to March 1986. He was a lawyer and human rights advocate who spent his life fighting dictatorship and injustice. He cofounded the Haitian League for Human Rights and earned deep respect both at home and abroad.

- Sylvio Claude, a charismatic preacher and educator who founded the Haitian Christian Democratic Party. Drawing strong support from evangelical communities, he boldly opposed corruption and dictatorship and was repeatedly jailed under Jean-Claude's regime. After Jean-Claude's fall, he became a leading voice for moral renewal and democratic change. But his growing influence also made him a target.

- Leslie François Manigat, a brilliant constitutional scholar who spent years in exile, teaching and writing about politics and history. He founded the Rally of Progressive National Democrats.

Each represented a different vision for Haiti's future—and a different set of fears for the elite and the military.

However, as election day neared in November 1987, the promises of the transition collapsed into horror. Despite enormous voter enthusiasm, with millions preparing to cast their ballots, the military allowed violence to erupt. Armed thugs attacked polling stations, killing voters in broad daylight. In one infamous incident at a school in Port-au-Prince, dozens were slaughtered. The election was canceled midday, leaving the streets soaked in blood and the people's hopes crushed.

The 1988 elections, hastily organized under military control, brought Manigat to power—but not through a credible democratic process. Voter turnout was abysmally low, and the military controlled the outcome from behind the scenes. Manigat's presidency was short-lived. On June 20, 1988, Namphy had ousted him in a palace coup, demonstrating once again that the military still held power. Though Manigat remained active in politics and ran for office again, he was never able to reclaim national leadership.

Coups, repression, and confusion marked the next few years. But the democratic spirit was not extinguished.

The Rise of Aristide and the 1990 Election

After years of false starts, Haiti finally held its first genuinely democratic election in December 1990. Against all odds, Jean-Bertrand Aristide, a former Salesian priest and fiery preacher from Port-au-Prince who advocated liberation theology, won with nearly two-thirds of the vote. He was the voice of the poor, dispossessed, and the brokenhearted. He called his campaign *Lavalas*, meaning *the flood*—a tidal wave meant to wash away the old order.

His victory stunned the elite and the military, which had backed Bazin once again. Aristide's campaign was built on the power of Haiti's urban poor and rural masses, who saw in him a moral figure uncorrupted by power or privilege. But just months into his presidency, in September 1991, Aristide was overthrown by a coup led by General Raoul Cédras. The short-lived democratic dream once again turned into a nightmare.

The Road to 1994

The military regime refused to step down, even after agreeing to international accords, such as the Governors Island Agreement of 1993. Human rights abuses worsened. In response, the United Nations authorized a US–led intervention.

In September 1994, American troops arrived. But the war was avoided. A last-minute diplomatic mission, which included former President

Jimmy Carter, persuaded Cédras to leave. Aristide was restored to power, and Haiti entered a new, albeit fragile, era of democracy.

The Second Fall of Aristide

The restoration of Aristide to power in 1994 was hailed as a turning point—a fragile rebirth of Haitian democracy. He served out the remainder of his first term until 1996, then returned to the presidency in 2001 after winning the 2000 elections. But this moment of hope would not last. In 2004, Aristide was ousted once again, under pressure from both domestic and foreign forces.

His second presidency was marked by growing unrest, accusations of corruption, and violent opposition from former soldiers and armed gangs. Aristide's supporters claimed he was trying to implement long-overdue reforms in land redistribution, education, and health care. His critics, many of them from the business elite and former military circles, accused him of authoritarianism and using gangs for political enforcement.

The tension reached a boiling point in early 2004. A rebellion began in the north, quickly spreading to other cities. As the capitol grew unstable, international pressure mounted. On February 29, 2004, Aristide was flown out of the country on a US military plane—what he later described as a "modern kidnapping." The US government insisted it was a voluntary resignation.

Once again, Haiti was left in the hands of a transitional government backed by foreign powers. The dream of democratic self-determination was again put on hold. And once again, the Haitian people were left to carry the burden of uncertainty and betrayal. As one Haitian proverb puts it, *Dèyè mòn gen mòn*—*"Behind the mountains, more mountains."* The journey was far from over.

What Endures—and What Hasn't

Between 1804 and 2004, Haiti saw countless revolts, interventions, and power shifts. But one thing has remained constant: the extraordinary resilience of its people. Despite everything—slavery, invasions, dictatorships—they have preserved their culture, faith, and sense of self.

Vodou has been a key part of Haitian identity. As scholar Patrick Bellegarde-Smith notes, "Vodou . . . is the glue that has held Haitian society together in times of chaos and despair." It embodies a deep connection to ancestors, community, and survival.

Haiti's elite families, meanwhile—descended from postindependence landowners and, later, business dynasties—have long held power. They have resisted reforms and manipulated politics to maintain their status. This has left most Haitians, particularly those in the countryside, excluded from the political sphere.

Even today, many of the colonial patterns remain. The divisions between the rich and the poor, as well as those between urban and rural areas and educated and uneducated populations, continue to shape the nation's politics.

A Fragile Rebirth

Haiti's path from revolution to democracy is neither straight nor smooth. It is a path cut through foreign interference, internal corruption, and social inequality. Yet at every turn, acts of courage, creativity, and resistance also mark it.

The republic declared in 1804 shattered the moral order of the colonial world. But what followed was a long and bitter struggle to turn revolutionary ideals into stable institutions. Haiti was burdened with debts it could never repay, isolated by powers that feared its example, and fractured from within by divisions born of slavery and race.

And yet, the spirit that overthrew Napoleon's legions never disappeared. It lived on in the fierce tenacity of Haiti's peasantry, in the sermons of liberation theologians, in the drumming of vodou ceremonies held under moonlit skies, and in the ballots cast for leaders like Aristide.

The United States–led restoration of democracy in 1994 was not a final victory but a hesitant return to possibility—a reminder that even in Haiti, the most embattled republic in the Western Hemisphere, history is still being written. As I mentioned earlier, in 2004, Aristide was ousted once again.

The next chapter will look beyond political events and into the bones of Haitian society itself. What keeps inequality in place? Who holds power and who is left behind? And how have ordinary Haitians endured—not just politically but spiritually, economically, and culturally—in a system that has so often failed them?

The answers lie in the structure of Haitian life. But as always in Haiti, the questions lead the way.

CHAPTER 3

The Social Background

What good is freedom if it cannot feed the hungry, teach the child,
or give the farmer a share in the harvest? Liberation without equity
is freedom half-lived.

—Epigraph by the author

Who belongs in Haiti? Why does a country born in triumph remain trapped in suffering? Why do so many Haitians still live without access to good schools, clean water, or a voice in their own future? And how can a nation that began as a bold declaration of freedom still be so divided along the lines of wealth, language, and geography?

These questions guide our exploration of Haiti's social background. The roots of the country's inequality extend far into the past: back to the revolution, colonization, and choices made in the fragile years following independence. This chapter tells the story of how Haiti's society was shaped not only by the colonial system it overthrew but also by the social hierarchies and political habits it inherited and re-created. Understanding these roots is key to understanding Haiti today.

The social condition of Haiti, from its noble birth in revolution to its modern struggles, remains burdened by colonial injustices and internal inequalities. What began as a bold and world-changing revolt against slavery and European domination soon hardened into a new kind of division. The formerly enslaved masses, those who had fought and bled for freedom, were pushed to the margins while a small elite quickly took control of power, land, and resources.

From 1804 onward, the island was a nation of winners who were not equally rewarded. After independence, the overwhelming majority of Haitians—formerly enslaved men and women—became the rural peasantry. Though they had secured liberty, they received little else: no schools, no support, no say in the new government. Meanwhile, many of the revolutionary leaders, including elite Black Haitians and mixed-race citizens (historically referred to as *gens de couleur*), rose to positions of influence. They formed a ruling class that often viewed the countryside with suspicion, even contempt.

This social divide has endured to the present day. Roughly 85 percent of Haiti's population lives in rural areas or impoverished urban neighborhoods, excluded from the basic tools of a dignified life—steady employment, quality education, health care, and political representation. As historian Laurent Dubois writes, "The masses who had won freedom were not given the tools to build a future. They were abandoned."[2]

For the peasantry, daily life remains as harsh as it was a century ago. Many rely on small plots of land, outdated farming techniques,

---

[2]Laurent Dubois, *Haiti: The Aftershocks of History* (New York: Metropolitan Books, 2012), 127.

and seasonal labor. Few have electricity, reliable roads, or running water. Most children do not finish school. In contrast, Haiti's small elite—comprising about 1 percent of the population—holds a disproportionately large portion of the nation's wealth and enjoys an annual per-capita income of nearly $120,000 in American currency. At times in recent history, they have controlled over 44 percent of the country's revenue. In rural areas, per-capita income has hovered around $40 in American currency a year.

At first glance, this might seem like a mere statistic—a grim marker of poverty. However, the gap between the rich and the poor in Haiti is not just about money. It reflects deeper historical, social, and political divisions that have shaped the nation's destiny since its birth in 1804.

I didn't fully believe this reality myself until I was an undergraduate student at the State University of Haiti. One day in class, our sociology professor, Frank L. Gilles—who would later become the adviser for my senior thesis on the Haitian press—gave us a group assignment. We were to travel to a rural area just a few miles outside of Port-au-Prince and spend a week studying the economic and social lives of the people living there.

What we saw and learned changed us.

Despite the proximity to the capitol, life in that rural community felt like a different world. We were shocked to discover just how accurate that forty-dollars-a-year figure was. We asked the locals how they managed to survive. What we found was a quiet story of resilience.

Many of the families we met, often large and extended, lived on what they referred to as *family land*. These were small plots passed down from generation to generation, tracing back to ancestors who had received land after Haiti's independence. On this land, they grew what they could:

bananas, mangoes, beans, potatoes, and other staples. What little they didn't consume themselves might be sold or traded in local markets. Occasionally, they would make a trip to the capitol to sell a small portion of their crops.

There were no cinemas, no internet cafés, no bustling storefronts. Entertainment came in the form of vodou ceremonies—community gatherings where music, dance, and spirituality brought people together. Their clothing was simple and functional. Sandals were common. A pair of name-brand sneakers or a new shirt from the city was a rare and cherished gift, often sent by a relative living and working in Port-au-Prince. Even a small bag of sugar or a tin of cooking oil could light up a household with joy.

That field trip was more than an academic exercise. It revealed to us the true meaning of survival in Haiti—not only the physical act of making ends meet but the cultural and familial ties that hold people together in the face of poverty. It was a lesson in endurance and in the dignity that exists even in the most overlooked corners of our country.

Again, this chasm between rich and poor is not merely economic; it reflects deep historical, social, and political fractures that have shaped the country's fate since its founding. Although current figures have changed, the period following the restoration of democracy in Haiti was marked by worsening economic conditions. Meanwhile, elite families live in guarded compounds in Port-au-Prince, send their children abroad, and own businesses tied to international trade and finance.

These aren't just economic differences—they're social and historical legacies. After the revolution, Haiti was isolated by former colonial powers, particularly France and the United States. France demanded an indemnity in exchange for recognizing Haitian independence, plunging the new nation into debt that crippled its economy for over a century. The debt and the need to appease foreign creditors compelled the Haitian state to prioritize its limited resources for tax collection, military upkeep, and elite urban life while neglecting the needs of the countryside.

Education in Haiti has long favored the privileged. Public schools are few and underfunded. Most instruction is in French, a language fluently spoken only by the elite. The majority of Haitians speak Haitian Creole, which was only officially recognized in education and government in the late twentieth century. Even today, French retains an aura of power and prestige while Creole speakers are persistently viewed as backward or uneducated—a painful echo of colonial attitudes.

In the twentieth century, Haiti's deep social divides were reinforced under the Duvalier dictatorships. François and his son, Jean-Claude, ruled with brutality, building a state that served the interests of a loyal elite while repressing opposition and neglecting development. Aristide, the former priest who emerged as a champion of the poor, attempted to reverse some of this legacy after being elected in 1990. One of his symbolic acts was to remove the faces of the Duvaliers from the country's currency, replacing them with images of heroes from the revolution. Yet despite these gestures and brief periods of reform, the economic and social conditions of the majority did not improve significantly. Since then, the value of the Haitian gourde has continued to decline.[3]

Attempts to reform this broken system through land redistribution, decentralization, and rural investment have mostly fallen short. Foreign aid programs and nongovernmental organizations have made significant contributions in certain areas, particularly in health and education;

---

[3]The value of the Haitian gourde has fluctuated significantly since the 1990s due to inflation, political instability, and currency devaluation. Alex Dupuy, *Haiti in the New World Order: The Limits of the Democratic Revolution* (Boulder, CO: Westview Press, 1997), 78–82; Robert Fatton Jr., *Haiti's Predatory Republic: The Unending Transition to Democracy* (Boulder, CO: Lynne Rienner Publishers, 2002), 103–105.

however, their efforts are often temporary, poorly coordinated, or insufficient to meet the scale of the need. As one report from the US Agency for International Development (USAID) noted, "Haiti suffers not from a lack of ideas, but from a lack of sustained commitment and capacity."[4]

Ultimately, Haiti's social structure remains haunted by the ghosts of its founding: a revolution that liberated the people but failed to transform the society. The peasants who defeated Napoleon's army never received justice. The wealth and wisdom of Haiti's countryside remain largely untapped while the narrow strip of elite privilege in Port-au-Prince continues to dominate politics and business.

A Nation Divided, A Future Undecided

The story of Haiti's social inequality is not just a matter of numbers—it is a question of national identity. Who is the Haitian state for? Who belongs at the table? And what kind of future can be built on such uneven ground?

To answer these questions, Haiti must face uncomfortable truths about how freedom was unevenly distributed after the revolution and how systems of exclusion were re-created in the shadow of slavery's end. Dismantling these inherited structures will require more than foreign aid or charitable projects. It demands bold political reform, investment in rural life, and a national reimagining of justice.

As we examine the political institutions that have perpetuated this inequality, we must remember that social progress and political change are inextricably linked. One cannot be reformed without the other.

---

[4]USAID Haiti Country Development Cooperation Strategy, 2014–2018.

CHAPTER 4

The Political Background

In Haiti, the ballot box has too often become a coffin.
The past reloads its rifles,
and the future is shot before it can speak.

—Epigraph by the author

What kind of freedom survives a dictator? What does freedom mean in a nation where elections are drowned in blood and the voices of the people are stifled by the shadows of rifles and whispered threats? What kind of democracy is possible in a land where the past refuses to die and those who challenge the old order often pay with their lives? In Haiti, the political past is never far behind. To understand the struggle for democracy, one must first walk through the corridors of fear, silence, and resistance built under authoritarian rule.

This chapter explores Haiti's modern political evolution, from the rise of the Duvalier dictatorships to the fleeting democratic experiments of the

1990s. It is a story not only of coups and constitutions but of power and its misuse—of those who wield it, those who resist it, and those who are crushed beneath it. In telling this story, we must also understand the men and institutions who shaped this era: the infamous Tonton Macoute, the tragedy of the 1987 massacre, the rise and fall of Aristide, and the Lavalas movement that promised redemption.

From Elites to Dictatorships

Throughout Haiti's postindependence history, political life was dominated by rivalries between Black and biracial elites. These factions often fought not to expand liberty but to concentrate power, leading to cycles of purges, insurrections, and authoritarian retrenchments. The state remained weak in its service to the people but strong in its ability to repress.

This dynamic reached terrifying new heights in 1957 with the rise of François. With a deep understanding of Haitian folklore, Catholic symbolism, and vodou beliefs, he projected himself as a messianic figure—the savior of the Black masses. But his real power came not from the divine but from the gun.

The Rise of the Duvalier Dynasty

No name casts a longer and darker shadow over modern Haitian politics than that of Duvalier. For nearly three decades, Haiti lived under the grip of a father and son who transformed the presidency into a throne—first François and then Jean-Claude. What began as a movement for Black pride and social justice would curdle into a reign of fear, superstition, and brutality.

François was not born a tyrant. He began life in 1907 in Port-au-Prince as a quiet, studious boy from a modest background. He trained as a physician and earned his nickname, Papa Doc, for his work combating tropical diseases like yaws in Haiti's rural countryside. There, far from the halls of Port-au-Prince's elite, François encountered the suffering and resilience of Haiti's poor Black majority—and he never forgot them.

But François was more than a doctor. He was a thinker steeped in the writings of Jean Price-Mars, Haiti's leading proponent of *noirisme*, which supported a racialist view of politics and culture. The Black Consciousness Movement championed Haiti's African roots and the dignity of its peasantry. François became a lifelong disciple of this ideology, and through it, he found both purpose and power.

François's first steps into politics came during the presidency of Dumarsais Estimé (1946–1950), one of the few Haitian leaders before him who sought to empower the Black majority. Estimé appointed François as director of public health and later as minister of health and labor. These posts gave him a taste of national influence but also exposed him to the jealousies and dangers of elite politics. When Estimé was overthrown in a military coup, François was forced into hiding. He would not forget that lesson, either.

In 1957, after a period of instability and a brief populist uprising led by Daniel Fignolé, François emerged as a presidential candidate. He styled himself as the Black Moses, promising to liberate Haiti's majority from generations of mulatto domination. With strong support from the countryside and covert encouragement from foreign powers hoping for stability, he won the presidency in a contested but decisive election.

Once in office, François moved quickly to centralize power. He sidelined the military, purged his enemies, and in 1964 declared himself "president for life." His private militia, the feared Tonton Macoute, enforced his rule through terror and intimidation. Political opponents were exiled, silenced, or disappeared. The state became his kingdom, and the line between politics and religion began to blur.

François wrapped himself in the symbols of vodou, presenting himself not only as a leader but also as a mystical father figure with divine authority. In his speeches, his portraits, and even the constitution, he built a cult of personality that equated loyalty to him with loyalty to Haiti itself. By the time he died in 1971, the country had been transformed—held captive by fear, superstition, and absolute control.

But the story didn't end there. It was only passed on—to his son.

In a move that stunned the world, François amended the constitution to allow the then-nineteen-year-old Jean-Claude to succeed him. That was a significant political mistake on the part of François: Jean-Claude inherited power without a clear vision. When Baby Doc took office in 1971, many hoped his youth would bring change. He was quiet, polite, and better educated than his father. But he lacked the fire, the cunning, and the ideological conviction that had driven his predecessor's rise.

Behind the scenes, real power remained with his mother, Simone Ovide Duvalier, and the old guard of François's inner circle. Jean-Claude played the role of president, but for years, he was little more than a figurehead.

Gradually, he grew into the role, though not in ways that would serve the country. His reign was marked by lavish spending, deepening corruption, and increasing alienation from the rural masses his father had once championed. His 1980 wedding to Michèle Bennett, a mulatto socialite from a prominent business family, symbolized a dramatic break with the Black Nationalist image the Duvalier dynasty had once cultivated. The extravagant ceremony cost millions and enraged the Haitian public.

Though Jean-Claude allowed more foreign investments and appeared to open Haiti to the world, the fundamentals remained unchanged. Opening Haiti to the world under Jean-Claude Duvalier meant encouraging foreign investment, expanding export assembly industries (such as textiles and electronics), promoting tourism, and cooperating with international lenders including the IMF and the World Bank. These policies tied Haiti more closely to the global economy but left political repression, economic inequality, and structural dependence unchanged. The Tonton Macoute continued to terrorize the streets. Poverty worsened. Schools and hospitals crumbled. By the mid-1980s, as protests swelled, the myth of Jean-Claude's invincibility began to crack.

Finally, on February 7, 1986, under enormous pressure from the Haitian people and quiet backing from the United States, Jean-Claude fled into exile in France, ending nearly twenty-nine years of Duvalier rule. He took with him millions in stolen state funds and left behind a broken country—bruised, impoverished, and desperate for change.

Jean-Claude returned to Haiti in 2011 after twenty-five years in exile, claiming he wanted to help. He was met not with applause but with lawsuits and accusations of human rights abuses and embezzlement. He died quietly in 2014, never having faced justice.

In the long shadow of Duvalierism, Haiti has struggled to rebuild democratic institutions, restore justice, and reestablish trust between its government and its people. The ghosts of the Duvaliers still linger—not just in memory but in the very structures and habits of Haitian political life.

The Tonton Macoute: A Government of Fear

To consolidate his rule, François created his personal militia in 1959 known as the Tonton Macoute, formally the Milice Volontaires de la Sécurité Nationale. Their name is derived from Haitian folklore about a boogeyman who kidnaps children.

The Tonton Macoute wore sunglasses and denim uniforms and often carried machetes or Uzis. They operated outside the law, becoming an omnipresent force of terror. Their mission was clear: eliminate all opposition to François. They were judge, jury, and executioner. According to historian Robert Fatton Jr., they helped create a "state of psychological siege" in which "no one could speak freely without fear of disappearing."[5]

From François's perspective, the pros of this institution included absolute loyalty, grassroots control, and a direct connection to the masses through fear. But for the Haitian people, the costs were staggering: Tens of thousands were killed or disappeared, civil society was silenced, and fear permeated everyday life.

1986: The Fall of a Dynasty

In 1986, after growing unrest, economic collapse, and pressure from abroad, Jean-Claude fled the country. But the system of repression did not vanish. A military junta composed of Duvalier loyalists stepped in.

The 1987 Election Massacre: Broken Hope

A national election was planned for November 29, 1987, and for the first time in decades, ordinary Haitians lined up to vote. There was hope in the air. But it was drowned in blood. Just hours into voting, armed men stormed polling stations.

[5]Robert Fatton Jr., *Haiti's Predatory Republic* (Boulder, CO: Lynne Rienner Publishers, 2002), 15.

At the Ruelle Vaillant voting center in Port-au-Prince, dozens of voters and poll workers were gunned down. Ballot boxes were destroyed. According to human rights observers, more than thirty people were massacred that day. The Inter-American Commission on Human Rights called it a "crime against democracy."[6] Historian Alex Dupuy notes, "It was a deliberate effort by elements of the military and former Macoutes to prevent the rise of a government that might challenge the old power structures."[7]

The Rise of Aristide

From this darkness, a new voice emerged. Aristide spoke directly to Haiti's poor. He denounced the elite, the military, and the remnants of Duvalierism. He preached liberation theology, a fusion of Catholic ethics and political activism.

Aristide was no ordinary politician. He lived among the poor. He rejected wealth. He called his followers to rise in dignity and resist injustice. In 1990, he ran for president under the banner of Lavalas—a movement meant to wash away the filth of repression and replace it with grassroots democracy.

His landslide victory was a cry from the masses. But Haiti's old powers refused to yield. In 1991, just eight months into his term, Aristide was overthrown by a military coup backed by elites and tolerated by international actors uncomfortable with his populist tone.

Lavalas: From Hope to Fragmentation

Lavalas was not just a political party. It was a mass movement—an idea of

---

[6]Inter-American Commission on Human Rights, *Report on the Situation of Human Rights in Haiti*, 1988.

[7]Alex Dupuy, *The Prophet and Power: Jean-Bertrand Aristide, the International Community, and Haiti* (Lanham, MD: Rowman & Littlefield, 2007), 48.

inclusion, justice, and local empowerment. It offered health clinics, literacy programs, and moral vision. But it also lacked structure. As internal divisions deepened and international pressures mounted, Lavalas began to fragment.

Aristide returned in 1994 under a US military escort and several conditions. He had to accept neoliberal reforms, privatizations, and foreign oversight. These compromises alienated parts of his base. Still, Aristide remained popular.

In 2004, amid renewed unrest, opposition protests, and allegations of corruption, Aristide was forced from office a second time. He claimed it was a kidnapping. The United States claimed it was a resignation. Either way, Haiti was once again thrown into crisis.

The People of Haiti: A Nation Beyond Politics

All too frequently, Haiti is seen only through the lens of its disasters and dysfunction. But the Haitian people are more than their suffering. They are descendants of Africans, Indigenous Taíno remnants, French colonists, and immigrants from Syria, Lebanon, Germany, and the Caribbean. Their culture is a blend of French and Creole languages, Catholicism and vodou spirituality, African rhythms, and Western ideals.

They are market women selling plantains in the dust. They are children reciting proverbs under mango trees. They are peasants who remember the names of their ancestors. And they are citizens who, time and again, have risked everything to cast a single vote.

Power and the People

Haiti's modern political history is not merely a string of failed governments. It is a story of a people seeking to reclaim the republic they birthed in revolution. The rise of Aristide and the Lavalas movement was not just a political event: it was a spiritual and social awakening. But the forces arrayed against them—old elites, militarists, and foreign actors—were powerful and patient.

To understand Haiti's political crisis is to understand the deeper clash between two visions: one where power is hoarded and one where it is shared. As long as the former remains dominant, Haiti's democratic dreams will remain fragile. But as long as its people remember the promise of 1804, the struggle for justice and dignity will never die. As Aristide himself once said, "You can kill the person, but you can never kill the dream."[8]

---

[8]This phrase echoes a motif found in the speeches of Martin Luther King Jr. and Billy Kyles, as well as Sophocles.

PART III

Conceptual Groundwork

CHAPTER 5

The Nature of Authoritarian Regimes

The tyrant's shadow is long.

It lingers in whispers,

in silence,

in bowed heads.

But the day comes when a people must remember

how to stand upright in the sun.

—Epigraph by the author

What happens when a country is ruled by fear instead of law? What lingers after the tyrant is gone? Can a democracy truly be born if the habits of dictatorship still fester beneath the surface?

These are not just abstract questions for political theorists. They are urgent, practical questions for anyone trying to understand the future of nations like Haiti—places where the struggle for democracy is not only about elections and institutions but also about overcoming ghosts of the past. To build a democratic future, we must first understand the undemocratic forces that haunt it.

Authoritarianism is more than just a word for harsh rule. It is a way of organizing power—a system that concentrates authority in the hands of a few and silences the many. In Haiti, like in many postcolonial societies, authoritarian rule has taken many forms: military juntas, strongman presidents, one-party systems, and regimes that promised order but delivered fear. Whether wearing civilian suits or military uniforms, these rulers often governed through control rather than consent.

Political scientist Juan Linz, one of the most respected voices on authoritarianism, described such regimes this way: "Political systems characterized by limited and nonresponsible political pluralism; devoid of a comprehensive guiding ideology (though often marked by distinctive mentalities); lacking significant political mobilization (except during specific developmental phases); and governed by a leader (or sometimes a small group) who wields power within imprecise yet predictably bounded limits."[9]

In simpler terms, authoritarian regimes limit opposition, centralize control, suppress dissent, and often rule with a vague yet firm grip on power. They may not always wear the harshest face, but their damage is usually long-lasting.

One of the most important questions to ask, especially in countries transitioning to democracy, is this: What remains when an authoritarian regime falls? Does the end of dictatorship automatically mean the beginning of a healthy democracy?

Katherine Hite, professor of political science at Vassar College, argues that it does not. In her research on authoritarian legacies, she explains that habits formed under such rule—habits of fear, silence, exclusion, and dependency—can persist long after the regime has fallen. These legacies

---

[9]Juan J. Linz, *Totalitarian and Authoritarian Regimes* (Boulder, CO: Lynne Rienner Publishers, 2000), 255.

act like invisible chains, binding the new democratic order to the logic of the old one.

She suggests that the weight of these legacies depends mainly on two things:

1. The duration and adaptability of the authoritarian regime—longer and more innovative dictatorships tend to leave deeper marks.
2. The nature of the transition to democracy—whether it was negotiated, abrupt, or imposed matters greatly in shaping the new system.

Authoritarian regimes often normalize things that democracy must reject:

- One-party or no-party dominance
- The exclusion of dissenting voices
- Routine repression
- Widespread human rights abuses
- Political habits rooted in coercion, not collaboration

When they fall, they leave behind more than ruined institutions. They leave psychological ruins—habits of distrust, political apathy, and moral numbness. These are harder to see but no less real.

Authoritarian regimes don't just suppress democracy; they shape the people, institutions, and expectations that make democracy possible. Even after the regime ends, its shadow may remain—etched into the walls of the palace, the silence of the press, the posture of the people.

To build a vibrant democracy, then, we must do more than change leaders. We must change the culture. We must do more than dismantle the machinery of dictatorship. We must unlearn its logic. This means challenging ingrained mentalities, fostering new habits of citizenship, and reawakening the moral imagination of the people.

This is especially true in a place like Haiti, where the past is never far from the present. The country's experience with authoritarianism under rulers like François and Jean-Claude Duvalier has left scars that still shape political life today. The story of gangs, violence, and institutional collapse is not separate from this history; it is a continuation of it.

And yet, there is hope. The fact that authoritarian regimes leave legacies does not mean that those legacies must last forever. They can be confronted, reformed, and ultimately replaced. But this takes time. It takes honesty. And above all, it takes courage.

From the Ashes of Tyranny to the Promise of Democracy

Having examined the inner workings and lingering effects of authoritarian rule, we are better prepared to ask a new question—not just what democracy is *not*, but what democracy *could become*. If dictatorship teaches us how easily power can be abused, then democracy must teach us how power can be shared, safeguarded, and humanized.

In the next chapter, we will turn to that brighter, more demanding vision—a vision not just of a political system but of a way of life built on dignity, participation, and trust. For Haiti and for all nations seeking to rise from the shadows of oppression, the journey is long—but it is a journey worth making.

CHAPTER 6

The Ideal of Democracy

Democracy is a dawn that must be defended each morning.
Its light is fragile, yet it chases away the night
if enough hands are willing to kindle the flame.

—Epigraph by the author

What does it mean to live in a democracy? Is it simply about casting a vote every few years, or is it something more profound, more demanding, and more beautiful? Can democracy survive in the face of division, corruption, and distrust? Can it grow in places like Haiti, where the weeds of authoritarianism, violence, and impunity often choke its roots?

These are not idle questions. They lie at the heart of every nation's journey toward justice and self-governance. Democracy, for all its flaws and frustrations, remains one of humanity's most powerful ideas: the belief that ordinary people can shape their destiny through institutions of fairness, equality, and law. And yet, for many societies, democracy is not a birthright—it is a fragile aspiration, constantly tested by internal strife, external manipulation, and the weighty inheritance of past regimes.

To understand how democracy can flourish, especially in a nation like Haiti, we must first examine what it truly entails—not as a slogan, but as a lived and living system.

More Than Just Elections

At first glance, democracy seems straightforward: government by the people, for the people. But dig deeper and it quickly becomes more complex. Yes, elections are essential—but they are only the beginning.

Economist Joseph Schumpeter famously defined democracy as a system where leaders are chosen through a competitive struggle for the people's vote. It's a tidy definition but far too narrow. As many modern thinkers argue, democracy cannot be reduced to the ritual of elections.

Real democracy requires more than just formal structures. It needs genuine participation, robust institutions, the protection of rights, and the freedom to challenge authority without fear.

Political theorist Robert Dahl gives us a broader vision. He defines democracy as a system marked by open elections, low barriers to political participation, meaningful competition, civil liberties, and public accountability. In Dahl's view, democracy must be an ongoing dialogue between the governed and those who govern—a conversation that includes all voices, especially those persistently silenced.

And then there's Benjamin Barber, a political theorist who paints an even richer portrait. For him, democracy is not just a system—it's a community. It's a shared project built by citizens who learn to work together, argue together, and take responsibility for their collective lives.

True democracy, he argues, embraces conflict—not by erasing it, but by managing it through cooperation and compromise.

This vision is especially vital in places like Haiti, where decades of authoritarianism, exclusion, and violence have fractured trust and silenced too many. Democracy in such settings is not just a political question. It's a moral one.

Civilian Power, Not Military Rule

Stanford University political science professor Terry Lynn Karl reminds us of a fundamental democratic requirement: civilian control of the military. This is no minor issue in Haiti, where the military has historically acted as a kingmaker—or king-breaker. When the gun overrides the ballot, democracy is always in danger. Civilian institutions must have the final say, not just in law but in practice.

Democracy demands that power be transferred peacefully, even when elections are hard-fought and outcomes disputed. Adam Przeworski, another leading scholar, emphasizes this very point: democracy doesn't eliminate conflict; it civilizes it. In a healthy democracy, winners govern and losers prepare to compete again. There is no revenge, no coup, no destruction of the game because one side lost. It is not about perfection; it's about process and patience.

Democracy and the Rule of Law

For democracy to thrive, it must be rooted in something more profound than popular will—it must be anchored in the rule of law. That means the law rules over people, not the other way around. When law is respected, justice has a chance. When the law is manipulated, freedom dies.

The rule of law requires:

- An independent judiciary that interprets laws without political pressure
- A transparent legal system that protects rights and ensures fairness
- Civilian oversight of police and military forces
- A free press that exposes corruption and defends public truth
- Perhaps most important, an educated, engaged citizenry that understands not only its rights but its responsibilities

Without these, democracy becomes a hollow shell—a stage play of freedom that masks oppression.

Conflict, Inclusion, and Civil Society

Democracy does not promise a world without conflict; it promises a way to handle conflict without violence or vengeance. This requires political systems that reflect a nation's diversity—ethnic, social, religious, and economic—so that no group feels permanently excluded or voiceless.

In Haiti, where historical wounds run deep and social divisions are sharp, building inclusive democratic institutions is not optional—it is essential. Electoral reforms, proportional representation, truth and reconciliation commissions, and the active role of civil society can all help build bridges where walls once stood.

Democracy also needs a vibrant civic life. Churches, unions, student groups, neighborhood associations—these are the spaces where trust is built, grievances aired, and solutions imagined. When civil society is weak, democracy has no heartbeat.

Democracy in the Digital Age

The digital revolution has added both promise and peril to the democratic project. On the one hand, social media and online platforms have empowered citizens to speak, organize, and hold leaders accountable. On the other hand, these same tools have been used to spread lies, stoke hatred, and manipulate public opinion.

Modern democracies must respond by:

- Promoting digital literacy to help citizens discern truth from deception
- Creating regulatory frameworks that protect against online abuse while safeguarding free expression
- Demanding transparency and accountability from tech companies whose platforms shape the public square

Democracy in the twenty-first century cannot ignore the digital battleground. It must learn to govern it wisely.

Democracy: A Living Promise

Ultimately, democracy is not merely a structure of government. It is a moral commitment. It rests on shared values: justice, dignity, equality, and mutual responsibility. It demands not just institutions but virtues: patience, trust, courage, tolerance, and accountability.

To defend democracy is not simply to vote. It is to live as a citizen, to believe in the worth of others, to speak when it is easier to be silent, and to act when it is easier to despair.

But democracy also rests on something even more fundamental: human rights. These are the foundation stones. Without them, democracy becomes a mask of tyranny. In the next chapter, we will explore those rights—what they are, where they come from, and why they must be defended. Only when democracy respects human dignity can it truly deliver on its promise.

CHAPTER 7

What Are Human Rights?

Human rights are the seeds of tomorrow's freedom.
Watered by courage, guarded by conscience,
they grow even in the stoniest soil—
promising that justice can take root
where injustice once reigned.

—Epigraph by the author

What does it truly mean to say we have rights? Where do these rights come from? Are they gifts from governments or more profound moral truths that no power on Earth can erase? And how do we protect these rights when the forces of fear, greed, or indifference threaten to overwhelm them?

In our modern world, few ideas carry as much moral weight—or as much confusion—as the concept of human rights. They are praised in speeches, enshrined in constitutions, and codified in international law. Yet for many people, their concept remains vague and abstract. What exactly are these rights we hear so much about, and why should they matter, especially in fragile democracies like Haiti?

To speak of human rights is to talk about the language of freedom, dignity, justice—and struggle. It is not a language born in comfort but forged in hardship: in the cries of the oppressed, the revolutions of the past, and the long march of civilization toward a more humane order. Human rights are not static artifacts—they are living principles shaped by the past, debated in the present, and vital to the future.

In this chapter, we'll examine the two primary categories of rights that continue to shape democratic life: classical rights—the ancient guardians of individual freedom—and positive rights, which are more recent in origin and seek to guarantee the basic conditions for a dignified life.

A Long Road to Dignity

Human rights, like democracy itself, are not the product of a single moment or mind. They are the cumulative inheritance of centuries of thought, struggle, sacrifice, and reform. From the Stoic philosophers of ancient Greece to the prophets of Scripture, from Enlightenment thinkers such as John Locke to modern revolutionaries, humanity has long grappled with a single, profound idea: every person matters.

Political philosopher Charles Taylor identifies two broad traditions that emerged from this long journey.

The first is the tradition of classical or "negative" rights—those protections against government overreach that shield the individual from intrusion or coercion. These include the rights to life, liberty, freedom of speech, freedom of religion, and a fair trial. These rights are like strong walls around the private spaces of the soul, ensuring that no ruler, however powerful, can violate the sanctity of the individual conscience.

The second tradition is that of positive rights—rights that seek not merely to shield individuals from harm but to guarantee them certain essential goods: education, employment, health care, and economic security. Positive rights ask a different question: How can a person be truly free if they lack the means to survive or to participate meaningfully in society?

These two visions are not necessarily opposed. Though they may occasionally pull in different directions, especially when economic policies or limited resources are at play, they are rooted in a common moral impulse: the belief that every human being is worthy of respect, protection, and opportunity.

A Heritage of Revolt and Reason

From England's Magna Carta of 1215 to its 1689 Bill of Rights, from America's Declaration of Independence to France's Declaration of the Rights of Man and Citizen, these milestones of political history have helped crystallize the idea that liberty must be protected by law.

These classical rights—those fundamental liberties that no government should violate—have deep philosophical roots:

- In Stoicism, we found the belief in the universal equality of all souls.

- In Christian thought, we encountered the conviction that each person is created in the image of God and is thus inviolably sacred.

- During the Age of Enlightenment, we saw the insistence that reason, conscience, and natural rights form the basis of any just political order.

These traditions converged in a simple but powerful claim: Some things must never be taken from the individual, no matter the will of the majority or the whims of the state.

To defend these rights is to draw a moral boundary around a person. It is to say, "Here, the law must stop. Here, the person stands free."

The Modern Struggle for Positive Rights

As societies became more complex, a new insight emerged: freedom without opportunity is an illusion. A person who is free in theory but lives in grinding poverty or systemic exclusion cannot fully exercise their liberties. Thus, positive rights were born—not to replace classical rights but to complement them.

These include:

- The right to education so that every person can think, speak, and act with confidence
- The right to work for fair wages so that dignity is not tied to privilege
- The right to basic health care and shelter so that no life is discarded for lack of means

While some fear that positive rights can be used to justify excessive state control or redistribution, they are not about charity. They are about justice—ensuring that no person is left permanently outside the gate of dignity.

Why Rights Matter Now

We live in an age of rising authoritarianism, mass surveillance, disinformation, and deepening inequality. Around the world, the rights once thought secure are being questioned, eroded, or outright attacked. In countries like Haiti, the situation is even more fragile. Here, political violence, systemic corruption, and the legacy of authoritarianism have made human rights not a luxury but a lifeline. To speak of rights in such a context is not academic—it is urgent.

The defense of rights requires more than courts or constitutions. It requires a culture of respect, a civic education, and a vigilant citizenry willing to speak truth to power and stand up for the vulnerable.

A Sacred Trust

Ultimately, human rights are not privileges granted by benevolent governments. They are solemn affirmations of the unyielding dignity of a human person.

Classical rights remind us that there are sacred spaces—of thought, belief, speech, and conscience—that no ruler may invade. Positive rights remind us that freedom must be nourished to survive. That without food, shelter, learning, and work, liberty can become a cruel joke.

In honoring both, we honor the whole human being, not just as a voter or a worker but as a creature of infinite worth.

To protect rights is to protect the fragile promise of democracy itself. In doing so, we do not simply preserve the past—we extend its promise into the future.

And now, having examined the rights that define our dignity, we must confront those forces that deny it. In the next section, we return to Haiti— not in theory but in lived reality, for it is there, in the struggle between violence and law, corruption and conscience, that the meaning of human rights is most severely tested. If democracy is the dream, then justice is the ground beneath it. And Haiti's path forward depends on how carefully that ground is nurtured.

CHAPTER 8

Major Players on the Political Stage

Haiti's political stage is crowded: generals and gang leaders, presidents and priests, diplomats and dreamers. Each actor writes a line in the unfinished script of the republic, where every scene feels like it could be the last.

—Epigraph by the author

Who holds the reins of power in Haiti's democratic struggle? Who shapes its future—and who stands in the way? What institutions, foreign and domestic, are helping to write the next chapter in the country's ongoing fight for justice and self-rule?

Democracy in Haiti has not been a straightforward march ahead. It has been a winding, turbulent drama—a contest not just between dictatorship and democracy but among a shifting cast of actors: state and nonstate, foreign and local, hopeful and hardened. Some of these players wield immense geopolitical influence. Others labor in relative obscurity, driven by principle and passion. Together, they form a vast and entangled network of forces shaping Haiti's fragile experiment in democratic governance.

The story of Haiti's political development is not only about ideas—it is about interests, institutions, and influence. And at each turning point, from the fall of the first Duvalier dictatorship in 1986 to the tumultuous elections and political crises of the twenty-first century, key players have emerged to either support or hinder the construction of a democratic order.

A Web of Influence: Foreign and Domestic

At the forefront of international involvement stands the United States government, which has consistently voiced support for democracy, human rights, and the rule of law in Haiti. Prominent among its institutions are the US president, members of Congress—particularly the House International Relations Committee[10]—and various agencies within the US Department of State, such as the Bureau of Democracy, Human Rights, and Labor, which annually reviews and reports on Haiti's human rights record to Congress.

Complementing these efforts are agencies like USAID, the US Information Agency, and the International Military Education and Training program. These bodies have promoted democracy through diplomacy, funding, education, and reform initiatives. USAID in particular has played a leading role in supporting electoral processes, judicial reform, and civil society development. It has also contributed to

---

[10]U.S. Congress, *History of House Committee Names*, "Committee on Foreign Affairs," *Congress.gov*, accessed September 22, 2025, https://www.congress.gov/help/committee-name-history. The committee was officially renamed the *Committee on International Relations* by H. Res. 163 (94th Cong., 1st sess.), March 19, 1975; the name reverted to *the Committee on Foreign Affairs* at the start of the 96th Congress, on February 5, 1979. The title "International Relations" was again used from 1995 until January 2007, when "Foreign Affairs" was reinstated and has remained in use since.

security sector reform, primarily through the training and equipping of the Haitian National Police.

However, recent developments have cast a shadow over USAID's future engagement in Haiti. Amid shifting US foreign policy priorities, rising domestic pressures, and mounting frustration over Haiti's persistent instability, funding levels for USAID programs are being reevaluated and, in some cases, reduced. The impact of this retrenchment could be significant. Without sustained investment in Haiti's democratic infrastructure, from courts to schools to civic groups, the gains of previous decades may erode under the weight of corruption, violence, and public distrust.

Building Civil Society: Nongovernmental Efforts

Outside the formal machinery of government, organizations like the National Endowment for Democracy play a crucial role. Through its four core grantees—the National Democratic Institute, the International Republican Institute, the American Center for International Labour Solidarity, and the Center for International Private Enterprise—the National Endowment for Democracy has supported a wide range of Haitian initiatives. These include civic education, independent journalism, grassroots organizing, and institutional transparency.

Yet for all their commitment, these efforts face daunting obstacles: limited resources, the omnipresent threat of violence, and deep-seated public cynicism. In a political climate where gang intimidation is rampant and the line between state authority and criminal enterprise is often blurred, the reach of civic actors is constrained by fear, fatigue, and fragile institutional partnerships.

The Watchdogs: International Human Rights Organizations

Groups such as Amnesty International, Human Rights Watch, and the United Nations Human Rights Council have been indispensable in documenting abuses, issuing alerts, and keeping Haiti's human rights crisis on the global agenda. They shine a light where shadows gather—reporting on political repression, extrajudicial killings, and the routine violation of due process.

Their work provides moral pressure and international scrutiny. However, even this spotlight is often dimmed by Haiti's systemic challenges, including a weak judiciary, limited enforcement capacity, and a pervasive culture of impunity. Documentation alone does not deliver justice, primarily when the institutions responsible for accountability are either absent or compromised.

Local Struggles, Local Heroes

Within Haiti, political and civil organizations have shown remarkable resilience. Groups such as the National Popular Assembly (later known as the National Popular Party), the Movement for the Installation of Democracy in Haiti, and the National Front for Change and Democracy[11] continue to advocate for democratic participation, government accountability, and social justice. Their efforts, however, are routinely undermined by a combination of structural weakness and existential threat.

The challenges they face are formidable:

- Armed gangs exerting de facto control over many neighborhoods and municipalities
- A judiciary riddled with corruption, incapable of delivering

---

[11]FNCD (Front National pour le Changement et la Démocratie), Haitian political coalition, 1990.

impartial justice

- A political class disconnected from the people, more beholden to foreign donors and private interests than to public service

In such an environment, democratic activism becomes an act of bravery and hope, a radical gesture.

A Theater of Persistence

Despite decades of involvement from global powers, waves of foreign aid, and the tireless efforts of countless Haitian patriots, the road to democracy in Haiti remains uneven and uncertain. It is a path riddled with setbacks, betrayal, and disillusionment—but not without courage, endurance, and vision.

The US government and affiliated institutions have provided support, but their efforts have often been piecemeal, reactive, or compromised by conflicting priorities. Organizations like the National Endowment for Democracy and its partners continue to empower underserved voices, yet they face immense challenges. International watchdogs deliver truth, but the machinery of justice remains slow. And local groups—those closest to the people—press on, caught between the promise of democracy and the reality of danger.

What emerges from this tangled landscape is not a tale of triumph nor one of total failure. It is a portrait of fragile persistence. Haiti's democratic promise has not been fulfilled—but it has not been extinguished, either.

As we move forward, the central challenge is this: How do we amplify and sustain the voices of Haitians who continue to fight for a republic rooted in justice, participation, and the common good? What structures must be built—not just funded—to outlast crisis after crisis? In the next chapter, we'll turn our attention to the fidelity of Haitian political actors, institutions, and the constitution, especially the one that was restored in 1994.

PART IV

Restored Democracy in Haiti: Governance, Institutions, and the Civic Spirit

The Civic Flame and the Fractured Republic: Haiti's Constitution and the Crisis of Democratic Practice

Konstitisyon se papye; bayonet se fè. (A constitution is paper; a bayonet is steel.)

—Haitian proverb

What makes a nation endure—steel or spirit? Can the force of arms ever replace the strength of civic faith? And what happens when the letter of the law survives but the soul of the republic begins to fade?

In Haiti, such questions are not mere abstractions—they are lived realities. Beneath the fragile shell of formal institutions lies a deeper battle: the struggle between power imposed and justice freely chosen. The Haitian proverb reminds us that iron may command obedience, but only shared conviction can sustain a people. Laws, no matter how fragile on paper, gain strength when inscribed in the moral consciousness of the nation.

Following the collapse of the Duvalier dictatorships and the long night of authoritarian rule, Haiti ushered in a new dawn with the adoption of the 1987 Constitution. It was not merely a legal document—it was a moral covenant, a collective act of hope. Born from wounds yet brimming with resolve, it aimed to replace the reign of fear with the rule of law and to ground the republic in liberty, dignity, and democratic participation.

The Promise and the Betrayals

The Constitution stood as a beacon. It forbade political killings, torture, and arbitrary detention. It guaranteed freedoms of speech, the press, association, and voting. It sought to constrain elite power and channel political life through democratic norms. Yet from the beginning, the return to constitutional governance was marred by opportunism, institutional fragility, and a civic culture still finding its footing.

After the US intervention in 1994 restored Aristide to the presidency following a brutal coup, the world dared to hope. But that hope was soon tested. Charismatic and emboldened, Aristide contemplated extending his term to make up for lost time spent in exile, a move that would have violated constitutional term limits. It was only under tremendous national and international pressure that he stepped back from the brink.

And then came René Garcia Préval. Préval was not a revolutionary firebrand. He was not a man of stirring speeches or dramatic gestures. He was, at heart, an agronomist—a man of the soil. Born in Port-au-Prince in 1943, he was raised in the lush rural commune of Marmelade. Educated in Belgium and Italy, he trained in agronomy and geothermal sciences. Exiled during the Duvalier years, he washed dishes and waited tables in New York before returning to Haiti with a quiet determination to serve.

Préval entered politics as a close ally of Aristide and briefly served as prime minister before being swept away in the 1991 coup. But unlike many who fell from power, he returned—not in defiance but through democratic election. In 1996, he became the first president in Haitian history to serve a full term and peacefully hand over power to his successor.

Préval's presidency was not without flaws. In his second term (2006–2011), he attempted to bypass Parliament and rule by decree during a time of legislative gridlock—an act that echoed the very executive overreach the Constitution was meant to prevent. Yet under intense civic and international scrutiny, he relented. In this, Préval revealed the paradox of Haitian democracy: fragile yet still functional, violated yet still capable of being corrected.

A Nation's Fragile Flame

Préval governed during one of Haiti's darkest chapters: the devastating earthquake of 2010 that claimed over two hundred thousand lives and leveled much of Port-au-Prince. He survived, but Haiti's institutions barely did. His administration was criticized for its slow and uneven response even as he remained a stabilizing figure, embodying quiet continuity when everything else seemed to collapse.

And yet during his presidency, the flame of civic virtue flickered. Elections were marred by fraud and violence. In towns like Kenscoff and Carrefour, polling stations were burned or attacked. Candidates like Henock Jean-Charles were assassinated. In 1999, the home of Ernso St-

Clair head of the Grand'Anse electoral department, was set ablaze for his defending the vote.[12]

Préval himself was not immune to the brutal cost of public life. His sister, Marie-Claude Calvin, was shot and her driver killed in a chilling reminder of how thin the veil of stability truly was.

The Constitution as a Challenge and a Call

Despite its disappointments, the 1987 Constitution remains Haiti's most vital symbol of civic aspiration. Its survival is due not to perfection but to its enduring power as a moral compass. It continues to call not to the ambitions of the powerful but to the better angels of the citizenry. It is a fragile flame—rekindled again and again by those who believe Haiti can be more than its past.

And Préval, for all his flaws, played a crucial role in keeping that flame alive. He governed not with grand illusions but with a kind of civic sobriety. He was no savior and he never claimed to be. But he understood what few others did: that democracy in Haiti would not arrive in a single moment of triumph. It would come, if at all, through patient cultivation.

Toward a Civic Renaissance

The path forward does not depend on strongmen or saviors but citizens. Democracy must be taught, practiced, and defended not only at the ballot box but in homes, schools, churches, and streets. It must be woven into the fabric of Haitian life.

International partners must abandon short-term crisis fixes in favor

---

[12]Reuters report (Dec. 13, 1999) summarized in U.S. Citizenship and Immigration Services, *Resource Information Center: Haiti*, entry for Dec. 10, 1999 (burning of the home of Ernso St-Clair, president of the Grand'Anse BED), archived Oct. 14, 2015. See also local coverage referenced in the same chronology (Haiti Online, Dec. 12, 1999),

of long-term investment in civic infrastructure. But above all, Haitians themselves must believe in the promise of self-government again.

Préval's life—quiet, grounded, resolute—offers a model not of perfection but possibility. He proved that one need not shout to lead and that dignity in public service can be a form of resistance against despair.

Let this chapter serve as both a warning and an invitation: a warning that democratic structures are meaningless without a democratic spirit and an invitation to reclaim that spirit through action, sacrifice, and shared responsibility. For though the Constitution is paper and the bayonet is iron, it is the fire of civic virtue, tended by hands like Préval's, that outlasts them both.

PART V

A Comparative View of Human Rights in Practice: Haiti and the Unfinished Promise of Human Rights

CHAPTER 10

Respect for the Integrity of the Person: The Sacred Worth of the Human Person

Guard the dignity of every person — and any nation can rise.

—Epigraph by the author

What does it mean to be free, not just on paper but in life? Can a country call itself a democracy when its people still live in fear? When a knock on the door after midnight is not from a neighbor but from a government agent? When people are jailed without charge, tortured in silence, or killed without cause?

For Haiti, these are not hypothetical questions. They are the real, lived questions of generations. In this chapter, we ask whether the most basic rights—the right to life, the right not to be tortured, the right to a fair trial—have truly taken root in Haitian soil. We compare the harsh realities under dictatorship to the more hopeful but still troubled years after the return of democracy in 1994.

This chapter focuses on the most essential rights, often called *negative rights* or *fundamental liberties*, because they are about what governments must *not* do: They must not kill their citizens, torture them, imprison them unfairly, or invade their privacy. These are not privileges. They are the bare minimum of a humane and just society.

We also examine how these rights are enshrined not only in Haiti's own Constitution but also in international treaties that Haiti signed in 1995—treaties intended to bind the nation to a new standard of justice.

But did they? And do they now?

What Are These Rights, and Why Do They Matter?

In 1995, Haiti ratified two major international human rights agreements:

- The International Covenant on Civil and Political Rights
- The International Covenant on Economic, Social, and Cultural Rights

These are binding treaties overseen by the United Nations. They require governments to respect the most basic human rights.

Here are a few key rights promised under the International Covenant on Civil and Political Rights:

- The Right to Life (Article 6): No one shall be arbitrarily deprived of life.

- The Right to Be Free from Torture (Article 7): No one shall be subjected to cruel or degrading treatment or punishment.
- The Right to Liberty and Fair Arrest (Articles 9–10): You must be told why you are arrested, receive a fair trial, and be treated with dignity.
- The Right to Privacy (Article 17): Your home, family, personal life, and reputation should be protected from government intrusion.

Haiti's constitutions—it has had more than twenty during its turbulent history—have echoed these promises. Yet the test is not in the writing. It is in the living.

Before 1994: The Age of Terror

During the Duvalier dictatorships (1957–1986), followed by military regimes in the late 1980s and early 1990s, the Haitian people lived under fear and brutality. Some of the most serious violations were:

- **Political Killings**
  Dissidents, journalists, priests, and even judges were murdered. Few investigations were ever launched. People such as *Gasner Raymond* and *Yves Volel* are remembered as martyrs of press freedom and justice.

- **Disappearances**
  Many who opposed the regime vanished. Some were never found. Others turned up dead, their bodies bearing signs of torture.

- **Torture and Inhumane Prison Conditions**

  Detainees were beaten, starved, and often denied medical care. Children were imprisoned with adults. Figures such as *Michèle Montas* endured both fear and physical abuse.

- **Arbitrary Arrests**

  The feared *Tonton Macoute* and army forces arrested people without warrants or trials. Being a journalist or religious leader was reason enough for imprisonment.

- **Violations of Privacy**

  Families were spied on. Homes were raided without cause. Letters and phone calls critical of the government could make someone a target.

This was not justice. It was governing by intimidation rather than law.

After 1994: A Fragile Hope

In 1994, democracy was restored to Haiti with the reinstatement of Aristide, backed by international forces. The world hoped this would mark a new chapter in Haitian history.

Some things improved. By the late 1990s, disappearances decreased, with politically motivated disappearances largely absent from international reports.

But other abuses continued:

- **Political Killings Did Not End**

  Even in the first months of Aristide's return, more than twenty politically motivated killings occurred. The assassinations of *Mireille Durocher Bertin* and *Senator Jean-Yvon Toussaint* showed that violence remained a political weapon.

- **Torture by Police**

  The International Civilian Mission, a joint effort of the United Nations and the Organization of American States, documented routine mistreatment by law enforcement, including beatings, water torture, and psychological abuse.

- **Arbitrary Arrests and Detentions**

  Political opponents and relatives of activists were jailed without charges. In some prisons, more than 80 percent of inmates were held without a formal accusation.

  Among the troubling examples of arbitrary detention during the early months of Aristide's administration was the arrest of former President Ertha Pascal-Trouillot. On April 4, 1991, just two months after she peacefully transferred power to Aristide following democratic elections, Pascal-Trouillot was arrested on vague and unsubstantiated charges. The government accused her of complicity in a failed military coup that had taken place in January 1991. This attempt sought to overturn the results of the very election that had brought Aristide to power.

Despite the gravity of the accusations, no formal charges were immediately filed. The government prosecutor, Anthony Alouidor, failed to provide any clear basis for the allegations. Instead, Pascal-Trouillot was publicly charged at the Port-au-Prince courthouse and then transported to Haiti's National Penitentiary. She was held overnight and subsequently placed under house arrest—a restriction that was lifted six days later, on April 10, 1991. The swiftness with which she was released suggests the absence of credible evidence and the politically motivated nature of her detention.

Pascal-Trouillot had served as Haiti's provisional president from 1990–1991, overseeing the nation's first truly democratic elections. She was also a legal pioneer: the first female attorney in Port-au-Prince, the first woman to practice law in Haiti's capitol, and the country's first female judge and Supreme Court justice. Her brief presidency marked the first time a woman of African descent had held executive power in any country in the Americas.

Her arrest—without clear charges, proper legal process, or a transparent judicial review—was not only a personal injustice but also a symbol of how easily the sacred worth of the human person could be disregarded in moments of political tension. It stands as a cautionary tale: Even those who dedicate their lives to justice and democratic governance are not immune to the abuse of state power. That such treatment was directed at one of Haiti's most respected legal minds speaks volumes about the fragility of human rights protections in times of political upheaval.

- **Lack of Fair Trials**

  Judges and prosecutors lacked independence. Corruption and underfunding crippled the courts. People spent years in jail awaiting trial—if they ever got one.

- **Illegal Searches and Privacy Violations**

  Police entered homes without warrants. Opposition figures remained under surveillance or threat.

Why It Still Matters

Though some abuses have declined, many of the same patterns remain. What changed is the language—dictatorships made no apology. Today, violations are cloaked in legality, committed in the name of national security or law enforcement. But their impact on human dignity is the same.

A democracy cannot thrive if people live in fear, if justice is for the few, and if dignity is just a word instead of something precious and honored.

The True Measure of a Republic

The strength of any republic lies not in its military, nor even in the ballots it casts, but in how it treats its weakest and most vulnerable citizens. Human dignity is not a favor a government bestows. It is a sacred trust that must be defended.

If Haiti is to rise, if its democracy is to endure, it must begin here—protecting people. Rights must not only be promised but practiced. Laws must not only be written but lived. And dignity must not only be invoked but felt in the lives of adults, workers, students, and all those who dream of something better. Until then, democracy in Haiti will remain a house built on sand—fragile, unstable, and always at risk of collapse.

Let it be said that the foundation of that house must be the sacred worth of the human person. Only then can the rest of the structure—elections, institutions, liberty—truly stand.

CHAPTER 11

The Fragile Breath of Freedom: Civil Liberties in Haiti's Struggle for Democracy

Freedom is not a flag to wave, but a breath to guard — lose it once, and the air grows thin.

—Epigraph by the author

Imagine living in a country where saying the wrong thing could result in arrest, where a peaceful protest might end with police beating down the crowd, where a journalist is silenced not by argument but by threats— or worse. Traveling outside your city, let alone your country, requires permission from a regime that fears your voice.

That was Haiti under a dictatorship. And even after democracy was restored in 1994, old habits proved hard to shake.

This chapter examines the state of civil liberties in Haiti before and after the fall of the dictatorship and asks whether the most fundamental freedoms that define a democracy have ever truly taken root. Civil liberties are not rewards handed out by governments; they are birthrights. The right to speak freely, to gather peacefully, to worship according to conscience, to move freely within one's country—these are the freedoms that let people think, dream, and organize for change. But they are fragile when power feels threatened.

What Are Civil Liberties?

Civil liberties are the fundamental rights and freedoms that protect individuals from government abuse. They allow people to express themselves without fear, to gather in public, to practice their religion, and to associate with others in a common cause.

Haiti pledged to protect these rights when it signed the International Covenant on Civil and Political Rights in 1991 and formally ratified it in 1995. This international treaty, overseen by the United Nations, commits countries to respect key freedoms. Some of the most essential articles include:

- Article 2 (1): Equal rights for all, without discrimination.
- Article 12: Freedom to move within your own country and to leave and return to it at will.
- Article 18: Freedom of thought, conscience, and religion.
- Article 19: The right to express opinions without interference.
- Article 21: The right to hold peaceful public gatherings.
- Article 22: The right to form associations, including political parties and unions.

These rights can be limited only under stringent circumstances—such as to protect national security or public safety—and only by law.

Before 1994: When Liberty Was Smothered

Under the Duvalier regimes and the military juntas that followed, civil liberties in Haiti were virtually nonexistent. The state ruled through fear, surveillance, and brute force.

Free Speech and Press Curtailed

In 1981, the government passed a chilling law: All news content had to be submitted to the Ministry of the Interior and Territorial Communities seventy-two hours before publication. Journalists who refused were harassed, censored, attacked, or killed. By the time of the 1991 military coup, independent media had largely disappeared, and many radio stations had shut down. Self-censorship became the only means of survival.

Peaceful Assembly and Association Banned

Protests and public gatherings were forbidden. If people dared to march in the streets or organize politically, they were met with violence. Activists were beaten, imprisoned, or disappeared. The mere act of gathering to discuss politics was seen as a threat.

Movement Restricted

Travel was tightly controlled, both within the country and abroad. Many political opponents had their passports confiscated or were outright banned from leaving the country. Others were forced into internal exile, cut off from their families, supporters, and safety.

In short, civil liberties weren't just restricted. They were annihilated. Haiti became a land where fear stifled speech and public life was dictated from the top down.

After 1994: A Glimmer of Light, a Shadow of the Past

When democracy was restored in 1994, there was hope that liberty would finally be more than a word in the constitution. Indeed, there were significant improvements. But authoritarian habits don't die easily. While some freedoms blossomed, others remained under siege.

Freedom of Speech and the Press

Journalists could now operate with far fewer restrictions. Foreign reporters were welcomed, and newspapers and radio stations once again voiced criticism of the government. But there were still troubling signs. In 1995, journalists covering police arrests were shoved and threatened. One local radio station was shut down after airing criticism of the authorities. Opposition media was sometimes harassed with bureaucratic roadblocks or denied licenses.

Freedom of Assembly and Association

Legally, citizens had the right to protest and to form groups. In practice, it was a different story. Police often broke up opposition meetings and arrested participants without warrants. A notable example occurred in 1996, when a political gathering in Port-au-Prince was raided and attendees were taken into custody. No legal justification was ever offered.

Freedom of Movement

Here, progress was evident. Citizens were no longer routinely denied the right to travel inside the country or abroad. Political exiles returned home. Passports were issued freely. After decades of restriction, this newfound mobility was a powerful symbol of regained dignity.

The Hard Truth: Freedom Needs More Than Laws

The revival of civil liberties after 1994 was genuine but incomplete. Old patterns still echoed through the halls of power. Freedom of the press existed but with boundaries. Public gatherings were technically allowed but often suppressed. Speech was freer, but critics of the state still faced consequences.

The painful lesson is this: liberty is not secured by law alone. It must be practiced by governments, protected by courts, and demanded by citizens every single day.

Liberty as a Living Flame

Haiti's journey toward civil liberty is a story of struggle, defiance, and unfinished promise. Under dictatorship, freedom was suffocated. Speech was silenced. Movement was restricted. Association was criminalized. The government's goal was not just to control people—it was to break their will.

The return of democracy in 1994 reopened the space for free expression, public assembly, and political organizing. Haitians could finally breathe a little easier. But even in this new era, the habits of repression proved stubborn. The press was freer but not always safe. Citizens could organize but not always without fear.

What this history teaches us is that democracy is more than elections. It is the daily right to speak your truth, to stand with others, to move without fear, and to live with dignity. These rights do not defend themselves. They must be defended by journalists who report the truth, by lawyers who demand justice, and by citizens who refuse to be silenced.

Let this chapter be a reminder: freedom, once won, is never permanent. It must be renewed and protected in every generation. In Haiti—and everywhere—democracy depends on it.

CHAPTER 12

Respect for Political Rights: Political Freedoms and the Fight for Self-Government in Haiti

When the ballot box is burned,

the people must light a brighter fire —

not to raze their cities,

but to forge their freedom.

—Epigraph by the author

A simple question, yet one that cuts to the very soul of a nation: Can we call a country democratic if the people cannot freely elect their leaders? If votes are stolen or ignored, if opposition is crushed or silenced, if ballots are burned and polling places attacked, what, then, remains of the promise of self-government?

In Haiti, this question has haunted generations.

Political rights—such as the right to vote, to run for office, to participate in public life—are not optional features of a democracy. They *are* a democracy. Without them, a government serves only itself, not its people. This chapter explores the long and painful history of political rights in

Haiti: how they were denied under dictatorship, how they were gradually reclaimed after 1994, and how, even now, they remain vulnerable to corruption, fear, and violence.

We'll also look at Haiti's obligations under international law. In 1995, the island ratified the International Covenant on Civil and Political Rights, a treaty that requires countries to guarantee core political freedoms. But as always, the gap between legal promises and lived reality remains wide.

What Are Political Rights?

Political rights empower citizens to take part in the governance of their country. They include:

- The right to vote
- The right to run for public office
- The right to take part in public affairs and decision-making

Under the International Covenant on Civil and Political Rights, which is overseen by the United Nations, these rights are spelled out clearly:

- Article 2 (1): All rights must be protected equally, without discrimination.
- Article 25: Every citizen has the right to take part in public affairs, to vote, and to be elected in free, fair, and regular elections.

These are not luxuries. They are the bedrock of democracy. When citizens lose the power to choose their leaders, they lose the power to shape their future.

Before 1994: Dictatorship and the Death of Democracy

For decades, political rights in Haiti were little more than an illusion. Under the brutal regimes of the Duvaliers, power was passed down like a family heirloom. Elections, if held at all, were staged performances— carefully choreographed to give the appearance of choice while offering none.

- **Presidents for Life**
  Both Duvaliers declared themselves rulers for life. No genuine elections were held. Opposition was banned. Political rivals were imprisoned, exiled, or executed. The government was not a public trust, but a private possession.

- **One Brief Glimpse of Hope**
  In 1990, Haitians were finally allowed to vote freely. The result was the landslide election of **Aristide**. But the celebration was short-lived. Just nine months later, in 1991, the military launched a coup, exiling him and plunging the nation back into fear and repression.

Throughout this era, political rights were not just ignored—they were violently suppressed. The people had no voice. Power belonged to those with guns, not votes.

After 1994: The Return of Democracy—on Paper

When democratic rule was restored in 1994 and Aristide returned to power with international backing, hope was rekindled. Haiti began to hold regular elections. In principle, the people were once again allowed to govern themselves.

But democracy is not just about holding elections—it's about the integrity of those elections. And in Haiti, that integrity remained deeply flawed.

- **Elections and Violence**

  The first rounds of elections after the transition were marred by violence, fraud, and intimidation. Polling stations were attacked. Ballots were burned. Voters were threatened. Some political groups, especially those linked to the former paramilitary force known as Le FRAPH (the *Front Révolutionnaire Armé pour le Progrès d'Haïti*), were excluded from political participation by mob pressure and vigilante action.

- **Progress with Painful Limits**

  From 1995 onward, elections were held at regular intervals. This was no small achievement in a country where, for decades, political transitions had happened only by coup. But meaningful political pluralism—the ability of all voices to compete fairly—remained elusive.

- **Culture of Fear**

  Even in the democratic era, violence, corruption, and threats continued to shape the political landscape. Many citizens feared retaliation if they supported the "wrong" candidate. Political opponents were intimidated or silenced. The line between politics and personal danger was never truly erased.

The Challenge: Democracy Without Trust

The vote is sacred, but only if it counts. In Haiti, the people have voted, but often without faith in the process. They have participated but often without protection. They have sought to shape their nation, but usually found the tools of democracy blunted by violence, corruption, or fear.

This reality raises hard questions:

- Does Haiti have elections? Yes.
- Are those elections always free and fair? More often than not, no.
- Do all citizens feel safe and empowered to participate in the democratic process? Not yet.

Until political rights are respected in practice—not just promised in law—Haiti's democracy remains incomplete.

The Power to Choose Is the Power to Be Free

True political freedom is more than voting every few years. It is the power to shape one's country, to speak without fear, to run for office without risking one's life. It is the heartbeat of democracy.

In Haiti, that heartbeat has long been faint: beaten down by dictatorship, revived by resistance, and challenged by those who still seek to control power through fear rather than fairness.

The Haitian people have shown extraordinary courage in reclaiming their political rights. But their struggle is not over. Political institutions must be reformed. Elections must be made safe and trustworthy. And above all, the state must protect the rights of *all* citizens, not just those in power.

As we reflect on Haiti's democratic journey, we return to the wisdom of the Haitian proverb *Konstitisyon se papye; bayonet se fè*. It means "A constitution is paper; a bayonet is steel."

Iron can be controlled. But only the will of the people can build a just and lasting peace. Only when rights are lived, when citizens cast votes without fear and leaders respect the outcome, can we say that democracy has truly taken root.

Let this chapter be a call: to guard the vote, to protect participation, and to remember that political rights are not given. They are claimed, defended, and kept alive by the people who dare to believe in a freer future.

PART VI

Discussion and Analysis: Gains, Shadows, and Enduring Struggles

CHAPTER 13

Democracy After 1994: Shadows That Still Haunt Haiti

We have seen dictators fall before.

We have danced in the streets,

only to march again in mourning.

Let the past no longer govern the present.

Let every ballot say,

'Never again.'

—Epigraph by the author

When the people celebrate the fall of a tyrant, when the ballots replace bullets and the constitution is restored, what happens next? Does democracy bloom immediately, as if on command? Or do the old habits return, dressed in new clothes, still whispering in the ears of the powerful?

Haiti has faced this question more than once.

In 1994, the international community assisted in restoring Haiti's democratic government after years of dictatorship and military rule. It was supposed to be a turning point. The Duvaliers were gone. The generals had stepped aside. The people had voted. But thirty years later, one must ask: has Haiti truly left authoritarianism behind?

This chapter explores the problematic legacy of dictatorship in Haiti's modern democracy. We look at what has changed since 1994 and what has not. Although the country now holds elections and maintains democratic institutions on paper, many of the attitudes, behaviors, and fears of the past still haunt its present.

Democracy Reborn—But Not Rooted

The Haitian Constitution, particularly the one adopted in 1987, is a powerful document, bold in its language and ambitious in its promises. It speaks of human dignity, justice, and the sacred right of the people to choose their leaders. But a constitution is not a magic spell. It must be lived, respected, and practiced.

- **Political leaders have treated the law as optional**
  During his second presidential term, Aristide was accused of trying to extend his mandate beyond what the Constitution allowed. Préval, too, issued decrees that raised eyebrows among legal scholars. In both cases, the temptation was the same: to bend the law rather than submit to it.

- **Elections have often lacked legitimacy**
  Since 1994, Haiti has held regular elections. But many of them have been marred by violence, fraud, boycotts, and fear. Political parties have pulled out. Ballots have been burned. Candidates have been killed. In such an environment, can the outcome truly reflect the will of the people?

These examples reveal a larger truth: While the *form* of democracy exists in Haiti, the *spirit* of democracy—its culture, its values, its moral commitments—is still dangerously weak.

Authoritarian Habits Die Hard

The dictatorship may have ended in 1986, but its shadow still looms. For over two hundred years—since independence—Haitian politics has, with disheartening regularity, been defined not by peaceful debate but by personal rivalry, vengeance, and violence.

- **Power is still seen as personal, not institutional**
  Too many leaders treat public office as a private throne to seize and defend rather than to steward with humility.

- **Opposition is viewed as an enemy**
  In a true democracy, rivals debate policies. In Haiti, political opponents are often met with intimidation, exclusion, or even assassination.

- **Justice is fragile, and the rule of law is selective**
  From arbitrary arrests to delayed or manipulated court rulings, the legal system is still often used to protect the powerful rather than to defend the people.

This continuity between past and present is not merely about weak laws. It's about a wounded political culture, one that has not yet fully embraced the habits of democratic life: compromise, accountability, mutual respect, and lawful restraint.

Haiti Today: A Nation Still Searching for Democratic Ground

Haiti bears the wounds of its past. Many of its political institutions are fragile. Its parties are often vehicles for personalities rather than platforms for ideas. Corruption corrodes trust. Violence, including from armed gangs, continues to shape the political climate.

Perhaps most painful of all, there remains a deep mistrust between those who govern and those who are governed. The elite are seen as self-serving and detached. The masses feel excluded, neglected, and betrayed. The state itself—its courts, police, and ministries—often feels like a distant force that is more feared than trusted.

These problems are not isolated. They are connected, rooted in a long history of authoritarianism, inequality, and political violence. And yet, there is something extraordinary in the Haitian people's endurance. Even after coups, corruption, earthquakes, and foreign interventions, they continue to protest, vote, speak out, and dream of a better nation. The hope of democracy, though battered, remains alive.

Beyond the Ritual of Elections

Let us be clear: holding elections does not make a country democratic. True democracy is not just about what happens on voting day—it's about what happens every day.

It is about respecting the rule of law. Accepting political defeat with grace. Debating rather than attacking. Protecting opponents rather than silencing them.

Haiti has taken essential steps since 1994. But it remains in the valley between dictatorship and democracy, still struggling to climb toward a future where human rights are not just legal texts but lived truths.

As we look ahead, let us remember:

Structures Do Not Save a Nation—People Do

And not just any people, but citizens who believe in justice, leaders who govern with restraint, and communities that refuse to forget the cost of lost liberty.

The Haitian people deserve more than a democracy in name. They deserve one rooted in conscience, sustained by culture, and honored in action. And that future, however distant it may seem, begins with truth, memory, and the courage to say: *"Never again."*

CHAPTER 14

The Road Ahead—A Sobering Yet Hopeful Path

Nations are not rebuilt by miracles but by memory and resolve— by people who refuse to surrender yesterday's dream to today's despair.

—Epigraph by the author

Can a nation rise from the ashes of its past? What does it take to build a democracy after a dictatorship? What kind of courage is required to plant hope where fear once reigned? And how does a people, long betrayed by those in power, find the strength to believe again?

Haiti stands at such a crossroads. The road behind is long, twisted, and shadowed by pain. The road ahead is uncertain—narrow, steep, and marked by both danger and possibility. For though Haiti has suffered more than most nations could bear, it has never lost its soul.

A People Unshaken

The Haitian people—fiery in spirit, poetic in soul—have endured centuries of hardship that would have broken many others. From the chains of slavery to the cruelty of dictatorship, from the devastation of earthquakes to the chaos of political collapse, they have not just survived. They have sung, prayed, danced, and resisted.

You hear their resilience in the voice of a woman selling fruit at dawn after losing everything in a flood. You see it in the hands of a father rebuilding his tin-roofed home stone by stone. You feel it in the cry of protest on the streets of Port-au-Prince when the promise of justice is again denied. As Haitian anthropologist Jean Price-Mars once wrote, *"Haiti's soul lives in its people."* They are the living proof that hope, even when battered, can endure.

A Civic Renaissance: The Path Forward

If Haiti is to move beyond its cycle of crisis and corruption, it will require more than institutions. It will require a transformation of civic life itself. The dream of democracy cannot survive on paper alone. It must be breathed into life.

Here is what that transformation must include:

- **The Law as a Living Ideal**
  The law must not be something used by rulers when it suits them and discarded when it doesn't. It must become a moral guide shared by all—a framework of justice, not just control.

- **Politics without Vengeance**
  The political game must shift from zero-sum battles to an actual

competition of ideas. There must be victory without arrogance and loss without retribution. This is the test of political maturity.

- **Civic Education for All**

  The Constitution must not gather dust on a shelf. It should be taught in schools, discussed in churches, quoted in market-places—made part of the moral language of everyday life. Every Haitian child should grow up knowing not just their history but their rights.

- **Accountability Beyond Elections**

  True democracy doesn't end at the ballot box. Leaders must answer to the people not once every five years but every day through independent courts, a free press, and a vigilant citizenry.

Most of all, the memory of past injustice must be transfigured not into cycles of revenge, but into an unyielding commitment to build something better.

A Difficult Truth: Democracy Never Fully Arrived

This book has traced Haiti's painful trajectory: from the shining promise of 1804, through the long darkness of personalist rule, to the fragile restoration of democracy in the 1990s. However, even that restoration, hard-won as it was, did not bring the profound change for which many had hoped. Though elections were held and constitutions adopted, the deeper moral foundation—trust between citizens and rulers, justice as a shared value, power as service rather than privilege—remained weak.

Many leaders governed not by law but by an old custom shaped by colonial legacies and authoritarian reflexes. The people, meanwhile, often remained excluded from the very democracy that bore their name. As Haitian political scholar Michel-Rolph Trouillot argued, *history is not simply a record of the past but a map of power.*[13] Haiti's past is still written in its present, and the abuses of yesterday echo loudly in the institutions of today.

Gangs, Power, and the Vacuum of the State

In the absence of strong, legitimate state authority, gangs have filled the void. What began as localized groups controlling neighborhoods have grown into shadow regimes that are sometimes better armed than the police and often more feared. These groups now influence elections, control movement, enforce their own rule, and even make political alliances. They are not just criminals; they are actors in Haiti's political economy.

This is the new face of power: fragmented, brutal, informal, and deeply rooted in inequality. When fear rules the streets, democracy cannot flourish. As this book has argued, we must disarm this system not only with weapons but with justice—addressing the poverty, exclusion, and betrayal that give it life.

Vodou: Spirit, Struggle, and the Soul of the Nation

At the heart of Haitian life lies vodou, often misunderstood abroad but deeply woven into the country's cultural and spiritual fabric.

Vodou, which some consider religion, is a cosmology, a history, a communal memory. It connects the living with the ancestors. It affirms dignity, celebrates survival, and helps people interpret a world where

---

[13]Michel-Rolph Trouillot, *Silencing the Past: Power and the Production of History* (Boston: Beacon Press, 1995), xxiii.

suffering and mystery coexist. During slavery, it was a shield of resistance. During dictatorship, it was a quiet form of spiritual rebellion. Today, it remains a source of both healing and conflict.

Sadly, like all things powerful, vodou has been manipulated. Some political leaders have co-opted it to cloak their rule in divine legitimacy. Others have scapegoated it, using superstition and fear to divide.

Yet its deeper meaning endures. It gives voice to the voiceless. It sanctifies the human soul in a world that often forgets it. *"Vodou is what holds us together when everything else is torn apart."*[14]

To understand Haiti's democratic struggle, one must understand vodou—not as folklore but as a living force of cultural identity and resilience.

Where Do We Go from Here?

Haiti's future hangs in a delicate balance.

The country stands between the memory of bondage and the dream of liberty, between the violence of gangs and the vision of justice, between forgotten promises and undying hope.

This book has not sought to romanticize Haiti's struggle, nor to despair over its failures. Instead, it has tried to hold both truths: the sorrow of the past and the stubborn hope of the present.

And so, we end this section not with a resolution but a call:

- Will Haiti finally become a democracy not just in form but in soul?

---

[14]Often-cited Haitian saying; no authoritative print source located. See Kim Wall and Caterina Clerici, "Vodou Is Elusive and Endangered, but It Remains the Soul of Haitian People," The Guardian, November 7, 2015; and *Associated Press*, "Shunned for Centuries, Vodou Grows Powerful as Haitians Seek Solace from Unrelenting Gang Violence," May 10, 2024.

- Will the people's voice rise louder than the gunfire of gangs?
- Will the Constitution become more than words and live in the hearts of its citizens?

These are not questions that scholars or politicians alone can answer. They are the daily task of the Haitian people. And though the road ahead is long, it is not empty.

In every act of faith, every vote cast in danger, every lesson taught, every injustice challenged, the people of Haiti remind the world who they are:

The children of revolution.

The keepers of Toussaint Louverture's *dream.*

The dancers on broken earth who still find rhythm in the dust.

Their democracy may be battered. But it is not dead.

Their spirit may be scarred. But it is not broken.

Let the world not pity Haiti—let it listen.

And may the next chapter, written not in fear but in freedom, finally do justice to the dream begun in 1804.

As we turn to the next section, we move from the ideals of law to the raw realities of power. For even as the Constitution calls Haiti to justice, another force has risen in its shadow: the armed gangs, the informal militias, and the brokers of violence who now hold sway over neighborhoods, elections, and lives. If the Constitution represents what Haiti could be, then the gangs represent what it must overcome. Democracy cannot thrive in fear. And so, we must face this crisis squarely—naming it, understanding it, and seeking ways to disarm it not only with force but with justice.

PART VII

Sacred Fear: Gangs, Vodou, and the Invisible Grip of Power

CHAPTER 15

A History of Gangs in Haiti

In Haiti, power has long worn two faces: one crowned, one masked.
The crowned face rules by decree, the masked by fear.
And yet, beneath both masks and crowns, the human spirit still
dreams of justice.

—Epigraph by the author

What happens when violence becomes normal? When the men with guns aren't strangers from afar but neighbors, cousins, even friends? What kind of democracy can flourish when fear is both physical and spiritual, when the danger is not just bullets but curses?

In Haiti, the path to democracy is not merely obstructed by poverty or corruption. It is blocked by an entrenched and often invisible alliance: political power, armed gangs, and deeply held beliefs. Power here does not reside solely in government buildings. It flows through back alleys, whispered threats, and vodou ceremonies meant to grant protection or strike fear.

This chapter examines the complex history of Haiti's gang phenomenon—how it evolved from the Duvalier dictatorships to the decentralized networks of today, its overlap with vodou practices, and its impact on both the daily lives and democratic aspirations of the Haitian people.

The Roots of Gang Power in Haiti

Gangs in Haiti didn't emerge out of thin air. They have long roots tied directly to political manipulation and state weakness. Modern history begins with the Tonton Macoute, the feared paramilitary force created by François Duvalier in the late 1950s. These men were not just brutal enforcers—they were often cloaked in the mystique of vodou, which François himself invoked to amplify his power. The Macoute were both executioners and symbols of sacred dread.

When François fell in 1986, the structure of violence did not vanish—it simply adapted. During Aristide's presidency in the late 1990s and early 2000s, a new wave of gang leaders, known as *chimères*, emerged. These armed men acted as unofficial extensions of political parties, enforcing loyalty, intimidating rivals, and manipulating entire neighborhoods.

After the devastating 2010 earthquake, the government's grip weakened even further. Gangs expanded their control, particularly in Port-au-Prince, filling the void left by absent institutions. According to researchers Athena Kolbe and Robert Muggah, gang networks grew more autonomous and more potent in the wake of disaster, preying on a population left with nowhere else to turn.

Vodou and the Spiritual Armor of Violence

To outsiders, the idea of seeking spiritual protection before entering battle might seem like superstition. In Haiti, it is both common and a serious concern. Many gang members regularly consult *houngans* (vodou priests) or *mambos* (priestesses) before acts of violence. They seek rituals to become bulletproof, curse enemies, or gain the favor of the spirits.

As anthropologist Elizabeth McAlister argues, vodou spirits are often drawn into political conflicts using ritual and song to mobilize their power in favor of one side or another.[15] These rituals serve as psychological armor—and sometimes as justification for brutality.

A young man from the Martissant neighborhood once told a Haitian human rights group: "Our boss took us to a houngan before we went to war with the other gang. He said the spirits would stop the bullets from touching us."[16] Another former gang member put it plainly: "You can't fight if the spirits don't bless you."[17]

In these communities, violence is not just a tactic. It is woven into a worldview where spiritual forces are seen as real participants in the power struggle.

Politicians and Their Muscle: A Deadly Partnership

Gangs are not just rogue elements operating outside the system—they are often part of it. Across administrations, Haitian politicians have forged

---

[15]Elizabeth McAlister, *Rara! Vodou, Power, and Performance in Haiti and Its Diaspora* (Berkeley: University of California Press, 2002), chap. 6, "Voices under Domination: Rara and the Politics of Insecurity."

[16]Testimony of a young man from Martissant, recorded by a Haitian human rights organization and cited in several YouTube documentaries on gang violence in Port-au-Prince, 2023–2024 —author's translation.

[17]Testimony of a former gang member, recorded in Haitian human rights interviews and featured in YouTube documentary reports on gang violence in Port-au-Prince, 2023–2024—author's translation.

relationships with gang leaders to protect votes, suppress opposition, and secure their grip on power.

During elections, gangs intimidate voters, threaten political enemies, and ensure turnout for their patrons. In exchange, they receive money, weapons, and a measure of immunity. Robert Fatton Jr., a prominent Haitian political scientist and professor at the University of Virginia, has described this arrangement as a "parasitic relationship" between the official state and unofficial, coercive networks.

In such a climate, democracy is a fragile performance. The ballot box is guarded not by law but by the man with the gun—and often, the priest behind him offering spiritual sanction.

The Everyday Cost of Fear

The damage done by gangs is not just political. It is profoundly personal and economic. In neighborhoods under gang control, leaders act as unofficial governors. They collect "taxes" from merchants, demand payments to cross certain streets, and dictate the flow of daily life.

Commerce stalls under the weight of fear. People are afraid to open their shops, travel to markets, or speak out. According to the International Crisis Group, gangs now control vast areas of Port-au-Prince, stifling economic life and limiting opportunity.

And then there is the metaphysical toll. Haitians live not only under the threat of bullets but also under the weight of curses. The fear is not only of death but of being spiritually marked, unprotected, or abandoned by the spirits. This sacred fear seeps into every aspect of life, eroding trust, discouraging civic participation, and making resistance feel futile.

Human Rights in a Landscape of Ritual and Rifles

How can human rights take root in a place where the law is flexible, the courts are weak, and justice is doled out not by judges but by gunmen and spirits?

The problem is not vodou itself, which remains a rich and essential part of Haitian culture and identity. The issue is its instrumentalization—its use as a tool of control and coercion. When sacred traditions are exploited for political or criminal purposes, they erode both moral order and democratic possibilities.

True democracy cannot flourish in such soil, not unless it addresses both the visible structures of violence and the invisible systems of belief. It must grapple with the power of the gun *and* the power of the ritual.

A Different Kind of Power

If Haiti's struggle teaches us anything, it is that democracy cannot be imported or imposed—it must be grown from within. That means confronting the harsh realities of gang control and spiritual manipulation, yes—but also recognizing the dignity, resilience, and faith of the Haitian people.

The road ahead will not be easy. But lasting reform will not come from foreign dictates or quick fixes. It must come from Haitians themselves—those who still dream of freedom, who still believe in justice, and who still find, amid the ruins, a reason to hope.

They are the ones who must reclaim both their traditions and their future. Only then can the dream of democracy be more than a distant echo in the mountains or a whisper in the alleyways. Only then can it become a living, breathing force—capable of transforming not just the state but the soul of a nation.

CHAPTER 16

Democracy, Vodou, and the Crisis of Haitian Identity

The drums that once called the enslaved to freedom still thunder in the Haitian night. Today they sound at the gates of the republic. The question is the same as it was two centuries ago: will they summon courage—or chaos?

—Epigraph by the author

What happens when a nation's spiritual soul becomes entwined with its political struggle? Can a society truly embrace democracy when its most enduring source of identity—vodou—is both a force of unity and a weapon of fear? Can belief, born of resistance and ritual, support the rule of law, or does it, in its unbounded form, sometimes undermine it?

These are not idle questions in Haiti, where the democratic dream is shaped by centuries of history and the unseen hand of the sacred. To understand the Haitian crisis, one must move beyond slogans of governance or electoral reform. One must enter the deeper, more complex terrain of culture, psychology, and belief where the spirits walk and politics listens.

This chapter probes the complex intersection between vodou and democracy in Haiti. It seeks neither to glorify nor to condemn but to ask honestly: How do we build justice in a world where spiritual forces are fundamental and political power is unstable? National identity is still emerging from the long shadow of enslavement and resistance.

Haiti's tale is neither clean nor straightforward: It demands clarity amid the entanglements of power, culture, and belief. Its crisis of democracy is profoundly complex—a knot of historical wounds, cultural resilience, and spiritual paradoxes.

Haitians endured nearly three centuries of brutal enslavement before organizing a revolution that culminated in their independence from France in 1804—the first successful slave revolt in modern history. It was not merely political will or military strategy that drove this revolution; it was also the spiritual force of vodou that united the oppressed. It served as the soul of the revolution—the sacred fire that emboldened resistance and solidarity, exemplified in ceremonies such as the famous gathering at Bois Caïman.

The gathering at Bois Caïman was more than a meeting—it was a night of destiny. Beneath a canopy of trees and stormy skies, enslaved Africans came together in secret, led by Dutty Boukman and a priestess of Vodou. They called upon the spirits, offered sacrifice, and swore an oath of unity. In that moment, scattered defiance became a single heartbeat, and the first sparks of the Haitian Revolution were struck—turning faith into fire and prayer into action.

Since independence, vodou has remained deeply woven into Haitian life, invoked in personal and political matters. Politicians seek legitimacy and protection through its rites; business owners consult its practitioners before new ventures. Across the nation, vodou endures—a presence, a belief, a cultural current that runs deep.

And yet, herein lies a great dilemma.

While many, particularly since the early twentieth century, have sought to elevate vodou to the status of religion, I cannot fully embrace that view. In his influential *Ainsi parla l'Oncle*, Price-Mars famously drew upon sociologist Émile Durkheim's definition of religion to argue that vodou, with its communal rituals and shared symbols, qualifies as a legitimate faith.[18] This view, noble in its cultural intent, sought to challenge the colonial narrative that reduced vodou to mere superstition and to affirm its place in Haiti's national identity.

Yet this argument rests more on structure than on substance. Though illuminating for understanding religion sociologically, Durkheim's lens bypasses the ethical demands religion must meet to serve as a foundation for justice and democracy. In its highest form, religion does not merely bind a community—it uplifts it through moral law, sacred texts, and a vision of human dignity. Vodou, by contrast, lacks a centralized scripture, a codified moral doctrine, or a consistent ethic of peace and forgiveness.

With troubling frequency, it is wielded not as a tool of healing but of harm: a vehicle for jealousy, revenge, and personal justice. In moments of conflict, spiritual retaliation is preferred over lawful mediation. Power is invoked not through dialogue or due process but through invisible forces summoned to curse, bind, or destroy.

In such a context, where fear, mysticism, and the potential for spiritual violence pervade daily life, how can democracy and human rights flourish?

---

[18]Jean Price-Mars, *Ainsi parla l'Oncle* (Paris: Imprimerie de Compiègne, 1928); Émile Durkheim, *Les formes élémentaires de la vie religieuse* (Paris: Alcan, 1912).

How can a just society take root when the passions of envy, fear, and revenge so easily redirect the moral compass?

These are the questions that haunt the Haitian democratic experiment. Until they are faced with honesty and courage, the path toward a stable and dignified political future remains fraught with peril. Vodou poses profound challenges to democratic development, yet its cultural and psychological importance remains too significant to ignore.

However, vodou's cultural and psychological importance cannot be ignored. As explored in *Vodou et névrose* and *Psychologie haïtienne: Vodou et magie* by J. C. Dorsainvil,[19] the practice is not merely a collection of mystical beliefs or esoteric rites. It is a comprehensive worldview deeply rooted in the Haitian soul.

Far from mere superstition, vodou acts as a religious and psychological framework through which the Haitian people interpret suffering, navigate trauma, and make sense of their reality. Dorsainvil demonstrates that vodou serves, in many respects, as a form of collective psychotherapy that channels pain and aspiration into symbolic expression through ritual, possession, and ceremony.

The lwa (spirits) are not distant or abstract; they are active presences in the devotee's life. The ceremonies, dances, and offerings are not idle performances but dynamic acts of memory, healing, and even resistance. In many communities, the vodou temple (or peristyle) is the only consistent institution offering social cohesion, moral support, and spiritual direction where the state has long been absent or indifferent.

In this light, any thoughtful analysis of Haiti's political crisis must account for vodou's dual role as both a spiritual refuge and a symbolic

---

[19]J. C. Dorsainvil, Vodou et névrose (Port-au-Prince: Imprimerie de l'État, 1940), and *Psychologie haïtienne: Vodou et magie* (Port-au-Prince: Imprimerie de l'État, 1936).

power system. Through vodou, one may trace the invisible loyalties, fears, and identities that shape political behavior, gang allegiance, and community order.

Ignoring its influence is to misunderstand entirely the terrain on which Haitian democracy must be built. Yet because of this power, vodou must be approached with cultural respect and critical discernment. The challenge lies in distinguishing the system's psychological and cultural depth from its moral ambiguity and susceptibility to manipulation, especially in the volatile nexus of politics, poverty, and spiritual authority.

The interplay among vodou, politics, and the struggle for democracy is undeniable. Postindependence, vodou offered spiritual solace and a framework for action, notably where foreign institutions lacked or were mistrusted. It provided a sense of agency and community. Yet this influence has sometimes been manipulated for personal and political gain, leading to actions at odds with democratic ideals and human rights.

Critics argue—and I agree—that the absence of a codified moral framework within vodou leaves it vulnerable to exploitation. Instances where it is used to settle personal vendettas or to exert control over others raise grave concerns about social cohesion and the rule of law.

Moreover, the entanglement of vodou and politics manifests in how some politicians engage with spiritual leaders to bolster their power. This dynamic blurs the lines between spiritual belief and political manipulation, potentially corroding democratic institutions.

In conclusion, while vodou is an inseparable part of Haiti's cultural identity and a testament to its historical resilience, its influence on contemporary politics and society presents opportunities and profound challenges. Price-Mars was right to defend the dignity of Haitian culture, but his vision of vodou as a religion, though historically significant, must now be reexamined considering the ethical demands of democracy. Addressing these complexities requires a nuanced understanding of vodou's multifaceted role and a steadfast commitment to building democratic institutions that honor cultural traditions while safeguarding human dignity and rights.

Haiti's crisis is not merely one of political dysfunction or economic despair. It is a crisis of identity—a deep, unresolved tension between the moral order required for democracy and the spiritual cosmology that shapes Haitian life. Vodou is not incidental to this story; it is central to it. It offers meaning, comfort, structure, and at times, peril.

The path forward must be one of discernment: embracing vodou's cultural depth and communal strength while rejecting its misuse as a tool of domination or fear. The question is not whether vodou should be part of Haiti's future but how it can be aligned with the ethical imperatives of justice, human rights, and the common good.

Only by facing this tension—openly, honestly, and with courage—can Haiti hope to forge a democratic identity that is both true to its past and worthy of its future.

PART VIII

Echoes of Empire: The Media in Haiti's Democratic Struggle

CHAPTER 17

The Colonial Roots of Haiti's Democratic Crisis

Evil is born not of ignorance but of knowing. When an empire sees the truth yet still chooses chains for profit—when cruelty is justified, power abused, and conscience stilled—the shadow of corruption falls across generations.

—Epigraph by the author

Why has democracy struggled to take root in Haiti? Why does a nation born in one of the most glorious revolutions of the modern age continue to wrestle with instability, exclusion, and fractured governance? Is the present crisis merely a failure of leadership, or does it reach back to the soil from which Haiti was born, deep into the brutal history of colonization and slavery?

To understand Haiti today, we must return to the age of empires when the island was not a republic but a colony—its people enslaved, its wealth extracted, its future mortgaged by violence. Haiti's modern political challenges cannot be separated from the long shadow cast by its colonial past. The struggle for democracy did not begin in the twentieth century. It started in bondage, in resistance, and rupture.

Saint-Domingue: The Plantation Colony of Wealth and Cruelty

By the late 1700s, the French colony of Saint-Domingue was the crown jewel of the Atlantic world—a producer of vast wealth through sugar and coffee, and a key engine of the French economy. Enlightenment thinkers praised liberty and equality in Parisian salons, even as their fortunes were funded by the enslavement of nearly eight hundred thousand Africans in the Caribbean.

Saint-Domingue operated under *Code Noir*, a legal framework that sanctioned extreme violence and systemic dehumanization. Enslaved men and women labored under punishing conditions, with life expectancy so short that the colony had to constantly import new captives from West Africa. In *The Making of Haiti: The Saint Domingue Revolution from Below*, historian Carolyn E. Fick describes the colonial regime not merely as exploitative but inherently unstable. From within the *maroon*[20] camps of escaped enslaved people and the secrecy of vodou ceremonies, a storm was gathering.

The cruelty of the system bred resistance. And resistance would soon erupt into revolution.

Revolution and Rupture

In August 1791, a coordinated slave uprising ignited a revolution that would alter the course of world history. It was the first and only successful

---

[20]The term *maroon* refers not to a color but to communities of enslaved Africans who escaped bondage and established independent settlements, often in remote mountains, forests, or swamps. These *maroon* societies—known in Haiti as *marrons*—preserved African cultural traditions, practiced vodou in secrecy, and waged guerrilla warfare against colonial authorities. They became potent symbols of resistance and freedom throughout the Americas.

slave revolt in the modern era. Leaders like Dutty Boukman (aka Boukman Dutty), Toussaint Louverture, Jean-Jacques Dessalines, and Henri Christophe waged a protracted struggle against the French, foreign invaders, and at times, against one another.

The Haitian Revolution, as Laurent Dubois argues in *Avengers of the New World*, was not merely an anticolonial war. It was a bold experiment in human liberation, a demand that freedom apply to *all*, regardless of race or birth. The revolutionaries envisioned a new kind of society, one founded on universal rights. Yet the price was staggering: cities burned. Plantations collapsed. The economy lay in ruins.

By the time independence was declared in 1804, Haiti had won its liberty at the cost of its infrastructure, its elite, and its unity. The revolutionary fire that had vanquished the empire left deep scars, and the nation that emerged was politically fragmented and economically fragile.

A Nation Born into Struggle: The Limits of Founding Documents

The 1805 Constitution, drafted under Dessalines, was among the most radical documents of its time. It abolished slavery, denounced racial hierarchy, and asserted Haiti's independence. Most strikingly, it declared that all Haitian citizens would be known as *Black*—a revolutionary move to reject the racial caste system of colonialism.

And yet the promise of this document soon collided with the realities of power. Dessalines crowned himself emperor, not president. After Dessalines's assassination, Christophe established a monarchy in the north while Alexandre Pétion governed as president in the south. The young republic quickly developed authoritarian habits. Suspicion of dissent, militarization of the state, and political rivalries became standard features of Haitian governance.

As Trouillot notes in *Silencing the Past*, the revolutionary dream was quickly constrained by the necessities of rule and the looming threat of foreign intervention. The ideals of liberty and equality were noble, but they were forced to operate within a world still shaped by empires and reactionary forces.

From Independence to Isolation

The world did not welcome Haiti's declaration of independence. The United States, France, and European powers viewed the new Black republic with hostility and fear. Haiti became a global pariah, isolated diplomatically and economically.

In 1825, France returned—not with troops but with terms. Under threat of invasion, Haiti agreed to pay a staggering 150 million francs in indemnity for the losses that former French slaveholders had suffered. This "debt of independence," although later reduced, crippled Haiti's economy for over a century. The payments forced Haiti into deep foreign debt and dependency. The nation's finances were mortgaged to European banks, and public resources were drained to satisfy the terms of its former oppressor. Independence had come with a heavy and bitter price.

Internal Divisions: The Fractured Republic

Even as Haiti faced pressure from abroad, internal divisions threatened its cohesion. Christophe's monarchy in the north clashed with Pétion's republicanism in the south. Tensions between the central authority and local autonomy, as well as between urban elites and rural peasants, deepened.

A small elite, often lighter-skinned and French-speaking, dominated the state. The rural majority—Creole-speaking, darker-skinned, and largely self-sufficient—was alienated from political life. Education, infrastructure, and opportunity were concentrated in the cities. The countryside was neglected and sometimes demonized.

Jean Casimir, in *The Haitians: A Decolonial History*, contends that Haiti's postindependence elite essentially "recolonized" the population. Though slavery had ended, a new form of exclusion took hold. The revolutionary masses who had fought for liberty were largely excluded from the nation they had created.

Land, the symbol of freedom and self-reliance for many former slaves, became another site of division. While the elites favored large estates and export agriculture, peasants carved out small plots, prioritizing autonomy over profit. The result was a persistent tension between a state modeled after European ideals and a society shaped by grassroots survival and resilience.

Democracy on Colonial Soil

Haiti's democratic crisis cannot be understood apart from its colonial inheritance. The authoritarian habits, the social divisions, the militarized state, the economic dependency—all are rooted in the long and brutal experience of colonization and enslavement. Haiti was born in revolution but never entirely escaped the architecture of empire.

And yet the Haitian people have never ceased striving. From the *maroon* camps to the ballots of modern elections, the will to self-govern persists. Democracy in Haiti is not an imported ideal—it is the unfinished business of a revolution that shook the world.

But for democracy to thrive, Haiti must reckon with its past—not only to remember but to repair. As long as colonial patterns remain embedded in the nation's institutions, language, and economy, the democratic experiment will remain fragile.

The future depends on this reckoning—on transforming the memory of revolution into a foundation for justice, inclusion, and enduring liberty. Only then can Haiti truly become what its founders dared to imagine: a republic of equals, free not only from chains but from the shadows that the chains have left behind.

CHAPTER 18

Shadows and Light—The Media's Role in Defending Haiti's Destiny

The past casts its shadow; the media must hold the light.
A nation survives not by forgetting its wounds,
but by remembering them with courage
and telling its story until it becomes its future.

—Epigraph by the author

What role should the media play in a nation's struggle for survival and self-definition? Can journalists be more than mere messengers? Can they become defenders of a nation's soul? In a country like Haiti, where history bleeds into the present and identity remains under siege, the answers to these questions are urgent and essential.

The past is not dead; it is not even past. This haunting insight by American novelist William Faulkner rings profoundly true for Haiti, a nation whose present struggles are inextricably linked to the threads of its revolutionary birth. In the long and mournful song of Haiti's history, the past is not merely remembered. It lives. It echoes. It directs. It is the shadow in the black-and-white portrait of the nation—not an accident of contrast but the very tension that gives the image its depth, dignity, and soul.

To move forward without memory is to stumble unthinkingly into ruin. When Haitians led the world's first successful slave revolt in 1804, they broke the iron chains of French colonial slavery—and thereby rewrote the possibilities of human freedom. Yet that monumental act was but the beginning of a long and unfinished journey. The battle for dignity, sovereignty, and survival continues, particularly in an international landscape where competition for resources, attention, and legitimacy are relentless.

Here, the Haitian media stand at a crossroads—not simply as observers but as potential catalysts. It is not enough for journalists and media institutions to report the news. In a country whose identity is perpetually challenged from within and without, the press must educate, inspire, and fortify the nation. Memory is not a luxury—it is a weapon. And those who control the channels of memory shape the nation's destiny.

The Media as a Moral and Civic Institution

The institutions of mass communication—newspapers, radio, television, film, and the sprawling digital landscapes of today—are the new battlegrounds for identity. As media scholar Stuart Hall reminds us, "The media are not the cause of modernity, but they have become the principal site in which modernity is articulated, struggled over, and experienced."[21] For Haiti, the media must become a steward of the national soul, not a passive mirror reflecting society's chaos but a lantern guiding it through shadowed paths.

---

[21]Stuart Hall, "Cultural Identity and Diaspora," in *Colonial Discourse and Post-Colonial Theory: A Reader*, ed. Patrick Williams and Laura Chrisman (New York: Columbia University Press, 1994), 392–403.

A Haitian journalist must see themselves not as a neutral scribe but as a teacher, a storyteller, and a protector of the people's memory. Scholars like Paulo Freire, in *Pedagogy of the Oppressed*, speak of education as a liberating force. The Haitian media must adopt a similar philosophy: Educate not by lecturing but by narrating, engaging, evoking pride, and awakening a sense of unfinished purpose.

Memory in Motion: History as Daily Bread

The struggle for independence, led by revolutionary leaders such as Louverture, Dessalines, Christophe, and Pétion, must not be relegated to dusty textbooks or annual speeches. These narratives should pulse daily through the veins of public discourse. They are more than history—they are identity.

Media outlets should invest in historical programming, including compelling documentaries, dramatizations, and public discussions, that does not merely list facts but stirs emotions, evokes pride, and offers a road map for what it means to be Haitian. As Trouillot argued in *Silencing the Past*, the writing and broadcasting of history is never neutral; it is a political act, one that either empowers or erases. The Haitian media must take a stance in favor of empowerment.

Building Solidarity and Showcasing Possibility

A nation is not destroyed solely by conquest—it also dies from within through division, apathy, and the erosion of common purpose. The media must become a herald of solidarity, not sentimentally but substantively. Campaigns should highlight examples of communal success, celebrate grassroots innovation, and spotlight everyday heroes, from teachers in remote villages to entrepreneurs in bustling cities.

Sociologist Benedict Anderson's concept of "imagined communities" helps us understand this task. Nations are built not just through borders or governments but through shared narratives and symbols. The media brings these narratives to life. If it neglects to do so, the national imagination withers.

Framing the Struggle in a Global Context

Time and again, Haitians are led to believe their struggle is isolated, exceptional, or irrelevant to the world. But history and political economy say otherwise. As philosopher Frantz Fanon wrote in *The Wretched of the Earth*, colonialism often mutates—it reappears not only through troops but through trade deals, exploitative aid, and cultural domination. The media must educate citizens on the modern forms of neocolonialism: how economic manipulation, foreign interference, and brain drain threaten Haitian independence just as surely as any army once did.

It must also encourage creative resistance. Today, a young Haitian coding a software solution or launching a sustainable farm is engaged in the same spirit of liberation as the heroes of 1804. That connection must be made explicit.

Education as a Form of Patriotism

Finally, the media must celebrate education, not as a weary duty but as a noble act of nation-building. In a globalized world, nothing is more revolutionary than a young Haitian woman mastering medicine or a young man studying environmental engineering. These pursuits are not escapes from reality; they are its transformation.

Public service campaigns, children's shows, reality programming, and cultural media must carry this thread subtly but consistently. As educator John Dewey insisted, democracy and education are inseparable; a functioning democracy depends on an informed and imaginative citizenry. Haiti's rebirth depends on both.

Lighting the Portrait of a Nation

If the past is the shadow in Haiti's portrait, then the media must be the hand that adjusts the light, bringing out the contours, the textures, the depths of what it means to be Haitian. It must remember not with melancholy but with fire. To forget 1804 is to betray it. To place it actively is to make the revolution a living guide — to carry its principles into today's struggles, giving direction and purpose to the unfinished work of freedom.

Freedom is never final. Sovereignty is never secure. And dignity is never inherited without labor. The Haitian media faces a choice: remain an idle chronicler of decline or rise as the bold herald of national awakening.

In this critical hour, Haiti needs less spectacle and more substance, less cynicism and more clarity. The pen, the microphone, the camera, the algorithm—all must be turned toward the service of national rebirth. Only then will Haiti move forward—wounded but wise, battered but unbroken—into the masterpiece of her own making, painted in bold strokes of shadow and light.

CHAPTER 19

The Media and the Crisis of Responsibility

*Every word spoken, every story told is a stone in the house of the
nation. Build with scandal and lies, and you raise only walls of
suspicion. Build with truth and wisdom, and you raise a 'lakou' — a
courtyard where a people may gather, learn, and live as one.*

—Epigraph by the author

Can a nation survive without moral guidance? What happens when
the most powerful communicators abandon their duty to educate
and unify? In Haiti's long and painful journey, the media have often
stood at a crossroads, capable of shaping national destiny or hastening its
unraveling. The time has come to ask: What kind of press does Haiti truly
need?

In a world overwhelmed by information, truth can be drowned. In
a society already burdened by crisis and distrust, a careless press can do
more harm than good. Haiti's predicament is not merely political or
economic—it is a crisis of cohesion, civic imagination, and shared moral

purpose. In such a moment, the role of the media becomes nothing less than existential.

Throughout its history, Haiti has been shaped not only by what has been done but also by what has been said and shared. The spoken word, the printed page, and the radio broadcast form the invisible architecture of national identity. Yet despite this extraordinary influence, the Haitian media has *persistently* failed to meet its noblest calling: to educate, elevate, and unify.

A Nation in Moral Crisis

Since its independence in 1804, Haiti has stood both as a beacon of freedom and a nation beset by fragmentation. The dream of a strong, self-sustaining republic has been repeatedly undermined by political instability and a chronic lack of trust. This fragmentation, rooted in Haiti's tumultuous origins, has been aggravated by a press that reflects society's divisions more than it repairs them. Instead of serving as a healing force, the media have often contributed to division, cynicism, and confusion.

Durkheim once wrote, "Society is not a mere sum of individuals. Rather, the system formed by their association represents a specific reality which has its characteristics."[22] In Haiti, this "specific reality" is one where the media wields immense influence yet repeatedly shirks its deeper responsibility.

Rather than fostering civic virtue, media content frequently revolves around scandal, conflict, and political gossip—*zin*.[23] Rarely does it speak the language of responsibility, solidarity, or hope. The Haitian public is often fed distraction instead of moral nourishment.

---

[22]Émile Durkheim, *The Rules of Sociological Method*, trans. W. D. Halls (New York: Free Press, 1982), 129.

[23]In Haitian Creole, *zin* refers to idle talk, gossip, or rumors—what in French is called *tripotage* or *tripotaje*. It often connotes the circulation of unverified stories, whispered intrigues, or sensational tidbits spread in the streets, markets, and now through the media. In political life, *zin* frequently distracts from substantive civic debate, reducing public discourse to rumor-mongering and spectacle.

What the Press Should Be

Traditionally, the press serves four functions: to inform, to offer opinion, to entertain, and to educate. Haitian media performs the first three with vigor but has largely neglected the fourth, particularly in its moral and civic dimensions.

In a country where formal education remains inaccessible for many, the media holds unique potential to serve as an alternative classroom. Especially in Haiti's oral culture, radio and spoken media are powerful platforms for public education. Imagine if every broadcast included lessons in history, civic duty, ethical reasoning, and national pride.

Freire argued that education must awaken critical consciousness. "Liberating education," he wrote, "consists in acts of cognition, not transferals of information."[24] Haitian journalists and broadcasters could embrace this model, understanding their role not as passive transmitters but as transformative educators.

A History of Missed Opportunities

The Haitian press dates back to *La Gazette de Saint-Domingue*, established in 1764. Over the centuries, the media landscape has evolved: radio in the 1920s, television by 1959, and now digital platforms. However, while technology has progressed, the moral mission of Haitian media has often lagged.

The post-Duvalier era presented a rare opportunity. Freed from the chains of censorship, the press could have reshaped national dialogue and deepened democratic culture. Instead, many outlets defaulted to sensationalism and political mimicry. A pivotal moment became a missed opportunity.

---

[24]Paulo Freire, *Pedagogy of the Oppressed*, trans. Myra Bergman Ramos (New York: Continuum, 1970), Chapter 2, "The Banking Concept of Education," p. 81.

As Trouillot warned in *Silencing the Past*, "History is not merely what happened; it is what is said to have happened." In Haiti, what is *said*—and *how* it is said—can either build or dismantle the national spirit.

The Press as Educator: A Moral Awakening

There is no reason the press cannot become a daily guide for the people—a modern-day *lakou (courtyard)* where ideas are exchanged, values taught, and a shared future imagined. But this requires a fundamental shift in vision.

The media must cultivate and celebrate virtue. It should highlight not just what outrages but what uplifts. It should showcase leadership, courage, and solidarity. Commentary must go beyond cleverness to embody wisdom and moral clarity.

Every day, the media should offer space for moral reflection, civic dialogue, and nation-building. It must help shape the habits, character, and conscience of a people. Philosopher Pierre Lecomte du Noüy argued that education is not merely the transfer of knowledge but the formation of moral character, rooted in enduring principles. Without that foundation, even the best instruction is shallow and society remains fragile. When the press becomes merely a business—or worse, a megaphone for discord—it betrays its trust. But when it reclaims its role as a bearer of values, it becomes one of the nation's chief architects of renewal.

Toward a Harmonious Social Life

Durkheim observed that education is the transmission of moral and social values from one generation to the next. A responsible press must take this charge seriously, especially in a fragile democracy. It should foster, as Emmanuel Mounier, the French philosopher and founder of personalism, put it, a "high psychological tension" toward the good—an active striving for moral elevation amid the pressures of communal life.

Social life is the web of relationships that binds people together. When those bonds are strong, a nation flourishes. When they decay through conflict, mistrust, and selfishness, society begins to unravel. We witness this unraveling in Haiti today, where interpersonal conflict and institutional decay are common.

The press could be a force for healing—a cultivator of trust, openness, and civic imagination. It could humanize rather than dehumanize, encourage compromise rather than conflict. But this would require a reorientation within the media, one that shifted away from superficial sensationalism and toward the sacred vocation of education.

Imagine if every media outlet dedicated time to promoting citizenship, history, ethics, and national responsibility. Such a transformation would not only enrich public discourse, it would help reweave the fabric of Haitian society.

Reclaiming the Public Soul

Haiti's future depends not only on its policies and elections but also on the inner life of its people. That inner life is shaped by what they see, hear, and come to believe. In this light, the media bears extraordinary responsibility.

This chapter is a call for a renaissance of purpose in Haitian media—for journalists, radio hosts, editors, and producers to reclaim the nobility of their craft and become mentors to the public, shaping citizens rather than just consumers. Only then can the press fulfill its highest calling: not merely to chronicle Haiti's crisis but to help resolve it. To become a steady flame in the dark, a voice of wisdom amid the noise, and a moral compass for a nation still striving for dignity, peace, and unity.

PART IX

From Revolution to Repression: Militarization and Media in the Democratic Age

CHAPTER 20

The Militarization of Power: Haiti's Armed Forces and the Erosion of Civil Rule

When the state learns to speak only in the language of force, it forgets the grammar of justice.
And a nation ruled by the barrel of a gun cannot teach its children the meaning of freedom.

—Epigraph by the author

What happens when the power to govern is rooted not in dialogue or consent but in force and fear? Can a democracy flourish when its guardians are soldiers rather than civilians? Haiti's story offers sobering answers.

Since its independence in 1804, the country has grappled with the question of who truly rules: the civilian or the military leader? While the revolution that gave birth to the world's first Black republic was a triumph of courage, it also left a legacy of militarized governance. Generals became presidents, political rivals were treated as enemies of war, and democracy, fragile and nascent, was often overshadowed by the march of boots and the click of bayonets.

This chapter traces Haiti's long and arduous journey with military power, from the early days of armed rule to the rise of paramilitary groups, from coups to foreign interventions, and into the lingering shadows left behind by decades of authoritarian control. It asks not only how Haiti's military shaped the state but how the state itself became, in many ways, militarized in spirit even after the army's dissolution.

As political philosopher Max Weber famously stated, "The state is that human community which successfully claims the monopoly of the legitimate use of physical force within a given territory."[25] But what happens when that force becomes illegitimate—when the sword forgets it is meant to serve the law, not subvert it?

The Rise of the Military in Postindependence Haiti

At its founding, Haiti was led not by lawyers or civic reformers but by military leaders fresh from the battlefield. Dessalines, the revolutionary general who declared independence in 1804, styled himself an emperor and governed through the structures of command and obedience he had known in war.

After his assassination, the country fractured. Christophe in the north erected a military monarchy while Pétion in the south led a republic that was more symbolic than civilian in its governance. In both regimes, the army was not a branch of the government—it was the government itself.

The political culture that developed was one of hierarchy, loyalty, and force. Bureaucracy was weak. Civilian life bent to military will. This early dominance of military figures in governance set a precedent: Holding power in Haiti often meant commanding soldiers, not citizens.

---

[25]Max Weber, *Politics as a Vocation*, in From *Max Weber: Essays in Sociology*, eds. H. H. Gerth and C. Wright Mills (New York: Oxford University Press, 1946), 78.

Summarizing the work of Haitian historian Michel Hector, we can say that the Haitian state emerged in the shadow of military rule—*born under the sign of the sword*, so to speak. Therefore, it is no surprise that the state has witnessed numerous coups.

Coups, Commanders, and the Collapse of Constitutional Rule

Over the next century and a half, the military's role in politics became entrenched. Haiti witnessed more than thirty coups between 1806 and 1986. Most changes in leadership were not decided at the ballot box but on the battlefield or behind closed doors in barracks.

Presidents like Faustin-Élie Soulouque and François C. Antoine Simon came to power through armed support and often fell the same way. Each new regime brought a fresh constitution—or the suspension of the old one. This cycle eroded any sense of legal continuity or civilian trust in democratic processes.

A culture of cynicism took hold. Government service became synonymous with coercion, not public service. Paraphrasing Fatton, we see that Haiti's state became prey to those who captured it rather than a vessel of national consensus or legitimate authority.

The Duvalier Dynasty: Paramilitary Terror and the Spectacle of Control

No era illustrates the fusion of militarism and authoritarianism more starkly than the rule of François Duvalier (1957–1971) and his son, Jean-Claude (1971–1986). François, though not a soldier, understood the logic of force. He weakened the traditional army and replaced it with his paramilitary force, the Tonton Macoute. This group, more feared than the formal military, operated with impunity and became the regime's iron fist.

The Macoute combined brutality with mysticism. Clad in dark glasses and wielding machetes, they invoked vodou imagery to project invincibility and fear. Their violence was not just physical—it was symbolic. By blending political terror with cultural spectacle, the Duvaliers created a regime of psychological warfare. This statement captures the essence of what Trouillot describes, especially in his analysis of the Duvalier regime's use of terror, spectacle, and vodou symbolism to control the population.

The army, now subordinate to the president, served less as a national defense force and more as an instrument of internal repression. Officers who defied the regime were imprisoned, exiled, or killed. The line between soldier, executioner, and sorcerer grew disturbingly thin.

After the Duvaliers: Military Coups and Foreign Boots

The collapse of the Duvalier regime in 1986 sparked immense hope for democratic renewal. But this hope was quickly tested. The military, under General Henri Namphy, stepped in to fill the vacuum, promising stability while maintaining control.

In 1991, Haiti's first democratically elected president, Aristide, was overthrown in a coup after just seven months in office. His ouster, orchestrated by military forces, provoked international outrage and eventually led to the 1994 United States–led intervention known as *Operation Uphold Democracy*. In a radical move, upon his return to power, Aristide dismantled the Haitian armed forces in 1995. He argued that the army had served only to suppress the people and perpetuate dictatorship. Some heralded this as a necessary step toward proper civilian governance. Others warned that abolishing the army without replacing its core functions—border security, disaster response, and national defense—would leave the nation vulnerable to external threats.

The Lingering Legacy: Militarism Without the Military

Though Haiti no longer has a formal standing army, the spirit of militarism lingers. In the absence of state-controlled security, gangs and informal militias have assumed the roles once played by the military: enforcing control, instilling fear, and shaping politics from the shadows.

These groups operate with their own hierarchies and codes, often backed by political elites. They act as both enforcers and power brokers, turning neighborhoods into territories and elections into high-stakes battlegrounds.

Debates continue about whether Haiti should reinstate a national army. Some argue that a professionalized force is vital for sovereignty and security. Others fear it would revive the authoritarian tendencies of the past.

The writing of journalist Amy Wilentz is right on point. She has repeatedly emphasized that Haiti's crises stem not from an absence of power or authority but from their abuse and from the absence of institutions that deliver justice, accountability, and the rule of law. In other words, Haiti's problem has never been a lack of force but a lack of justice.

Breaking the Cycle, Reclaiming Civil Rule

The challenge for Haiti is not simply to banish the military—it is to dismantle the mindset that power is earned through command, not consent. True democracy requires more than elections; it demands a civic culture in which legitimacy flows from the governed, not from the gun.

Rebuilding the nation means investing in civilian institutions: a fair judiciary, a professional police force, and local government structures that reflect the will of the people. It also means confronting the psychological scars left by generations of militarized rule. The task is not only political. It is moral and cultural. Haiti must learn, at last, to govern with laws rather than threats, with hope rather than fear.

As the Haitian proverb goes, *Tout moun se moun*—"All people are people." A democratic state begins with that simple truth.

CHAPTER 21

The Media's Sacred Task—Guiding Democratic Renewal

When truth is drowned in rumor, a nation gasps for breath.
The press must rise as prophet and sentinel,
speaking truth unbought and unbowed,
calling rulers to account and citizens to courage.

—Epigraph by the author

I n a nation seeking to rise from the ashes of its suffering, what should be the role of the press? Is it merely a mirror, reflecting the tremors and tempests of daily events? Or might it be something nobler—a torch in the darkness, a schoolhouse for the soul, a guardian of the republic?

In Haiti, these questions are not the province of ivory towers; they are vital to our survival. When the channels of communication become polluted with rumor and spectacle, when truth is drowned in the clamor of faction, what hope remains for civic unity?

The press in Haiti is not merely a business or a tool; it is a vital institution. It is a sacred trust—a moral pillar upon which democracy itself must lean. Let's use this faithful and powerful paraphrase of Czech statesman Václav Havel's eloquent words: the word is the most powerful weapon humanity has. And in Haiti's land, torn by silence and distortion, the need for honest, illuminating words has never been more profound.

Reclaiming the Press as Guardian of Truth

The first and highest duty of the media is to tell the truth—not fragments of it, not the convenient or popular version of it, but the whole and honest truth.

In an era marked by half-truths and manipulated narratives, Haitian journalists must stand like the prophets of old: unyielding, unbought, unafraid. They must resist the siren call of scandal and spectacle and instead labor at the demanding and noble craft of truth-telling. For truth, though often uncomfortable, is the only firm foundation on which a democratic house can be built.

In a country where trust seems nonexistent, it will be challenging to make it a reality. Truth is always uncomfortable, even for those who vehemently proclaim they love it and make it their mission to fight for it. Yet it is precisely this painful truth that our nation needs most—one that restores trust, guides conscience, and speaks not to passions but to judgment.

Journalism as Civic Education

The news must not be a mere parade of catastrophes, nor a stage for demagogues. Instead, it must become a national academy where citizens learn their rights, their duties, and the workings of their government. In a country where many lack access to formal education, the media becomes the chief instructor in the affairs of the republic. It must explain, patiently and without condescension, how laws are made, what a constitution means, and how power is to be held accountable. In this sense, the press is a schoolmaster of the people, not with a rod, but with reason.

Here, the vision of Freire comes to mind. Education, he wrote, should awaken "critical consciousness"—the power of individuals to understand and transform their world. The media in Haiti must rise to this pedagogical task, planting the seeds of a thoughtful, questioning, and civically engaged citizenry.

Giving Voice to the Voiceless

Democracy flourishes only when the least among us are heard as clearly as the greatest. The Haitian media must become the trumpet of those long silenced: the peasant in the field, the mother in the roadside market, the youth in the alleyways of forgotten towns. Their stories, too, are the nation's story. Their suffering, their courage, and their aspirations must be drawn from the shadows and brought into the bright light of public concern.

As Indian philosopher Amartya Sen has taught, democracy depends not merely on institutions but on inclusive discourse. When the voices of the excluded are heard, justice takes root. When they are ignored, the nation shrinks in soul. Let the media remind us that democracy is not only about elections or parliaments; it is about shared destiny and mutual recognition. And let no Haitian be deemed invisible to the national imagination.

Dismantling the Culture of Violence

The inheritance of militarism in Haiti is not only written in the chronicles of coups and uniforms. It has taken root in the very imagination of the people. Too often, the strongman is lionized. Too frequently, the gang leader is portrayed as a folk hero.

The media must cleanse this image. Let it cease to glorify the man with the gun and begin to uplift the man with the book, the woman with the broom, the youth with a plan. The quiet labors of peace-builders, educators, and reformers must be honored with the same attention once given to those who ruled through fear.

This is no small transformation. But it is a necessary one, for a culture that praises violence cannot long sustain freedom. The press must become a mirror that shows not what we are but what we must become.

Building a Culture of Dialogue

If democracy is the rule of persuasion over force, then public discourse is its beating heart.

Radio, television, and the new digital platforms must not merely broadcast opinion; they must host reasoned debate. Let the airwaves become arenas where citizens contend not in anger but in argument; not in shouting but in reasoned exchange.

A new political culture must be sown—one that prizes negotiation over confrontation, community over faction, and ideas over slogans. Just as a child must be taught to read, a citizen must be trained to listen, to question, and to speak with respect. In this way, the media may prepare the soil for a more mature and peaceful republic.

Cultivating Hope, Not Just Outrage

It is not enough to expose corruption. It is not sufficient to denounce failure.

The press must also become a herald of hope. It must shine its light on every honest mayor, every faithful judge, every thriving school, clinic, or village council. These are the living seeds of a new Haiti, and they must be seen and celebrated.

Hope is not the denial of reality—it is the defiance of despair. As author Rebecca Solnit has beautifully written about hope: "It is an axe you break down doors with in an emergency." Let the press wield that axe with care and courage.

In a weary land, good news is not a luxury. It is a necessity.

The Pen and the Republic

Long ago, the town crier did not ring his bell only to warn of danger. He also called the people to work, to worship, and to rejoice. Today, the Haitian journalist must do likewise. He must call his nation not merely to attention but to action. She must remind her people that this battered republic is not condemned to failure but invited to greatness.

Let the printing press, the radio wave, the television lens, and the digital page be wielded as instruments of national healing. Let them sing of justice and summon the people to virtue. And let those who practice the craft of journalism do so with the gravity of priests, the steadiness of teachers, and the hope of builders.

If, as the adage says, the pen is mightier than the sword, then let it be drawn not for vengeance but for vision—not to wound but to awaken.

The task is excellent. But so, too, is the dignity of those called to it.

PART X

Resistance as a Democratic Tradition: Civil Society and the Press

CHAPTER 22

The People's Struggle—Civil Society, Protest, and Accountability

Every protest is a hymn, every shout a prayer.

Haiti's resistance is a chorus centuries old—

sung by enslaved people, peasants, priests, and poets.

Even in the darkest nights,

the song of freedom rises,

carrying the promise that dawn will come.

—Epigraph by the author

Can a people continue to hope when their government repeatedly fails to meet their needs? What becomes of a nation when its institutions falter but its citizens refuse to surrender? And can resistance—steadfast, creative, and courageous—become the very soul of democracy?

In Haiti, the answer is yes.

If the Haitian state has often betrayed its citizens through corruption, neglect, or outright repression, its people have not betrayed themselves. From the era of colonial slavery to today's crises of governance, ordinary Haitians have time and again risen to challenge injustice, demand dignity, and assert their right to shape their destiny. In this land of revolutionary beginnings, protest is not just defiance—it is inheritance. It is the flame passed from Louverture to the streets of Port-au-Prince, from the peasant *piket* (militia) to the PetroCaribe hashtag.

This chapter explores the deep roots and enduring role of civil society—the networks of community organizations, faith groups, intellectuals, and ordinary citizens who fight not with weapons, but with words, songs, courage, and the dream of a better Haiti. Through a historical and cultural lens, we'll witness how protest in Haiti is not mere opposition. It is a sustained moral calling.

The Roots of Resistance: From Revolution to Rural Rebellions

The Haitian Revolution (1791–1804) was the first successful slave revolt in world history and the foundation of a Black republic born from struggle. But that founding fire did not die with the Declaration of Independence. It set the tone for a political culture where resistance would become a national characteristic.

In the decades following 1804, the elite-led central governments often sought to revive aspects of the plantation economy. In response, rural peasants resisted fiercely. Across the nineteenth century, *pikets*—local armed militias made up of farmers and ex-soldiers—rose in protest against unjust taxation, forced military service, and land seizures.

These rural uprisings were not aimless outbursts. They were grounded in local values and traditions, shaped by communal justice systems and spiritual rites. Political dissent was often expressed through vodou ceremonies, religious festivals, and oral storytelling—vehicles that carried messages of resistance across generations.

"Everyday life can be political," writes anthropologist James C. Scott, who studied peasant resistance globally. Haiti's peasants lived this truth daily.[26]

These movements, in essence, were rural democracies in action—challenging distant rulers with drums, machetes, and the collective memory of a revolution that had promised them more.

Intellectuals, Educators, and the Pen as Weapon

If peasants carried the spirit of resistance in their bones, Haiti's writers, teachers, and journalists carried it in their pens. They have long been the nation's conscience, raising uncomfortable truths in the face of repression and intellectual laziness.

Anthropologist Anténor Firmin, writing in 1885, dared to confront the racist science of the day. His treatise, *The Equality of the Human Races: Positivist Anthropology*, rejected European theories of Black inferiority and proclaimed the intellectual and moral dignity of all people, especially Haitians.

Price-Mars would later champion *indigénisme*, calling Haitians to embrace their African roots, language, and religion not as marks of shame but as sources of identity and pride. Vodou, for him, was not superstition but the cultural heart of the nation.

In the literary world, Jacques Roumain's 1944 novel *Masters of the Dew* told the story of peasant struggle with poignant realism and profound social critique. Underground newspapers, samizdat-style pamphlets, and impassioned public speeches were often the only platforms available to challenge tyranny.

---

[26]James C. Scott, *Weapons of the Weak: Everyday Forms of Peasant Resistance* (New Haven: Yale University Press, 1985), xvii.

For countless Haitian intellectuals, the written word was not a luxury—it was a duty. It was, to paraphrase Haitian writer Lyonel Trouillot, more than an act of civic courage; it was an act of heroism.

The Church and the Streets: Liberation Theology and Grassroots Mobilization

The 1970s and 1980s saw a surprising new engine of resistance: the church.

Born in the parishes but radical in its vision, the Ti Legliz (little church) movement emerged from the global tide of liberation theology—a Christian current emphasizing the gospel's call to free the poor from economic and social bondage. In Haiti, Ti Legliz became a sanctuary and organizing hub. Priests, nuns, and laypeople began holding literacy circles, community assemblies, and health workshops. Faith was no longer passive. It was an active, political, and deeply personal experience.

The traditional alignment of the church with the ruling elite began to fracture. Figures like Aristide started preaching not only spiritual salvation but also political deliverance. "The people must not suffer," he said from his pulpit—and they listened.

Throughout his work on liberation theology, particularly regarding the moral and political duties of Christians in contexts of injustice, Brazilian theologian, philosopher, writer, and former Franciscan friar Leonardo Boff expresses the idea that being Christian is about taking a stand for justice, even when it is dangerous. In Haiti, it was often deadly, but the faithful did not flinch. This spiritual revival evolved into a powerful civil movement, laying the groundwork for the mass protests that would ultimately topple the Duvalier regime.

Protest in the Face of Repression: From Duvalier to Aristide

By the early 1980s, the brutality of Jean-Claude had pushed Haiti to the brink. But the people—students, laborers, women, and clergy—pushed back harder. Protests swept through the country. Despite the Tonton Macoute, the feared paramilitary enforcers, ordinary Haitians took to the streets with chants, placards, and prayer. In 1986, Duvalier fled. The people had won.

But their victory was fragile. The 1990 election of Aristide, a fiery priest of the poor, was a triumph of grassroots mobilization. Yet he was soon overthrown in a military coup. Repression returned. Still, the people did not retreat. Throughout the 1990s and early 2000s, civil society kept the democratic flame alive by organizing, educating, and resisting. Women's groups, such as Fanm Yo La and SOFA (La Solidarité Fanm Ayisyèn), expanded the struggle, linking it to campaigns against gender-based violence, inequality, and exclusion.

The lesson was clear: in Haiti, democracy is not a gift—it is a fight.

Civil Society in the Twenty-First Century: NGOs, Youth Movements, and Digital Activism

The devastating 2010 earthquake ushered in a new phase for Haitian civil society. International aid poured in, accompanied by a surge in nongovernmental organizations (NGOs). Many of these groups became lifelines, providing essential services where the state was unable to do so.

Organizations such as Réseau National de Défense des Droits Humains began monitoring human rights violations, publishing reports, and pressing public officials to act lawfully. Others opened schools, clinics, and legal aid centers.

Meanwhile, a new generation rose—young, digital, and fearless.

Between 2018 and 2021, the PetroCaribe Challenge movement erupted. Sparked by outrage over billions of dollars allegedly stolen from public funds, thousands of Haitians, mostly youth, took to social media and the streets. With hashtags like #KotKobPetroCaribeA ("Where is PetroCaribe money?"), their demands for justice became viral and visceral.

Yet challenges remain. Many NGOs are tied to foreign donors, which can shape their mission and limit their independence. Fragmentation among civic actors can dilute impact. And in a society racked by gang violence and political instability, activism is often perilous.

Throughout his work, Sen reminds us that a society's freedom is best measured by how well it allows its citizens to speak. Haiti's civil society has never stopped speaking loudly, bravely, and often at significant cost.

The Spirit of Resistance as Democratic Hope

Civil society in Haiti is not perfect. It is fractured, underfunded, and often endangered. But it is alive. And it is the best hope for a democratic future.

The Haitian people—through churches, classrooms, newspapers, marches, WhatsApp groups, and whispered songs—have refused to remain silent. Their resistance is not reactive. It is visionary. It imagines a Haiti ruled not by fear but by participation, not by exploitation but by justice.

Haiti's struggle has never been derivative, never a borrowed script. It is a drama written in its own blood, its own hope, its own defiance. Across centuries, through chains and revolutions, betrayals and rebirths, it has carried its identity not as an imitation but as an origin. This land is not an echo of other countries. It is its own voice, speaking with the cadence of its history and the timbre of its struggle. This land is Haiti.

In a nation persistently overlooked, civil society remains the keeper of the flame. And from that flame, still flickering, may come the light of renewal.

CHAPTER 23

Fighting with Grace—The Press and the Art of Constructive Resistance

To resist without destroying is the highest discipline of a free people.
In Haiti, where hope has so often been betrayed,
the press must be the compass that points the way—
turning anger into action, grief into courage,
and the scattered cries of a nation into a single, defiant chorus:
We will not be silenced, and we will not lose ourselves.

—Epigraph by the author

What does it mean to resist without destroying? Can protest be both powerful and peaceful, both fierce and noble? And in a time of profound crisis, can the media be more than a mirror? Can it become a mentor?

In Haiti's ongoing democratic journey, these questions are not merely theoretical; they are a matter of practical concern. They cut to the very heart of national survival. Resistance is everywhere: in the chants of protestors, in whispered prayers, in the determined march of ordinary citizens who refuse to be silenced. But unless that resistance is guided—given form, purpose, and discipline—it can devour itself.

This chapter explores a vital idea: the press as an architect of constructive resistance—resistance that builds rather than breaks; resistance that redeems rather than ruins.

The Spirit of Resistance as Democratic Hope

Haiti's history is carved with struggle, and its present trembles beneath the weight of betrayal. Yet its spirit endures. From remote mountain villages to the bustling streets of Port-au-Prince, Haitians have never surrendered to silence. They resist not merely to survive but to proclaim a vision of life where dignity, justice, and shared participation are sacred.

This resistance is not just reactive—it is creative. It is a dream of democracy forged in sacrifice and sustained by collective memory. This spirit echoes the moral vision of theologian Reinhold Niebuhr, who emphasized perseverance and moral struggle in the face of despair.

The press, standing as both witness and participant, must now evolve into a strategic builder of this democratic dream.

The Media as the Guardian of Constructive Spirit

All too frequently, the raw energy of popular resistance has been hijacked by opportunists or steered toward chaos. Demagogues have turned crowds into mobs; righteous anger has dissolved into senseless destruction. As history has shown, rage without refinement becomes poison.

Here lies the responsibility of the media: not to suppress rebellion but to shape it, refine it, and elevate it. The press must become educator, strategist, and reconciler—offering a model of resistance that is disciplined, principled, and purposeful.

As Václav Havel put it (paraphrased), hope is not the conviction that something will turn out well, but the certainty that something is worth doing, no matter how it turns out. [27] The press must sustain that certainty.

Strategic Messaging: Teaching the Difference Between Destruction and Defense

In moments of upheaval, the difference between destruction and defense can be razor-thin. It is the press's role to clarify that difference. It must remind the public that protecting democracy requires more than passion— it requires wisdom. Through clear messaging and meaningful stories, the media must teach that civil resistance in a democracy includes:

- Defending voting rights
- Preserving the independence of the judiciary
- Demanding accountability from elected leaders
- Maintaining a peaceful protest with clear, constructive goals

Examples matter. The media can amplify the stories of quiet heroes:

- A teacher who instills civic values in the next generation
- A nurse who treats both protestors and police with equal care
- A priest who preaches peace without surrendering truth

Such narratives demonstrate that resistance can illuminate rather than incinerate. They provide moral blueprints for action.

---

[27]Václav Havel, *Disturbing the Peace: A Conversation with Karel Hvížďala*, trans. Paul Wilson (New York: Vintage Books, 1990), 181–82.

Building Alliances: A Media That Mobilizes, Not Isolates

The press must not speak alone. It must build deliberate partnerships with civil society institutions. These alliances transform media from a solo voice into a civic chorus.

Examples include:

- Partnering with schools to create engaging and accessible civic education materials shared through radio, online platforms, and community gatherings
- Collaborating with religious communities on moral messages rooted in nonviolence, dignity, and justice
- Working with artists and musicians to elevate cultural expressions of hope and resistance—songs, murals, plays, and poems that proclaim democratic values

In this way, the press moves beyond commentary. It becomes a conductor of civic symphony, harmonizing resistance with wisdom and grace.

Encouraging Local Watchdogs and Micro Voices

A healthy democracy cannot be guarded solely from the capitol. Its defense must be local, grassroots, and participatory. The press can nurture a culture of citizen journalism, empowering Haitians everywhere to be truth-tellers and watchdogs:

- Community radio stations can train youth to report on local governance, education, and human rights.

- Mobile media units can travel to rural areas not merely to broadcast but to listen, engage, and amplify unheard voices.

As Scott argued, the most powerful resistance often comes from "the hidden transcript"—the everyday speech and action of ordinary people in private spaces. The media can bring this into the light.

Sustaining Hope in the Face of Fatigue

Every movement must battle exhaustion. Resistance without hope becomes an empty ritual.

Here, the media must become a fountain of endurance, a storyteller of victories and perseverance:

- Anniversary specials that honor civic milestones—past elections won, oppressive policies overturned, or moments of collective triumph
- Profiles of perseverance—ordinary citizens who, despite fear or poverty, continue to act justly
- Spiritual reflections offered by respected figures, linking democratic struggle with themes of redemption, divine justice, and human dignity

In doing so, the media becomes more than a reporter. It becomes a keeper of sacred memory, ensuring that resistance is carried forward as both a duty and a hope.

Resisting the Temptation of Cynicism

The gravest danger to democracy is not always violence. It is despair—the slow erosion of belief that change is possible. Cynicism kills movements by convincing people that nothing matters.

The media must resist this temptation. It must:

- Critique without mockery
- Expose corruption without fatalism
- Challenge injustice without bitterness

Let it remind the people that democracy, like love, is fragile, but worth the labor. It must say: do not surrender hard-won gains to those who thrive on chaos. Progress may be slow and incomplete, but it is real—and it is ours to defend.

The Press as a Midwife of Democracy

Haiti is not a blank slate. Its people have dreamed, sacrificed, and struggled too long to begin again from ashes.

The democratic achievements—halting, fragile, imperfect—must be defended with vision and grace. The press must become a midwife of renewal, aiding in the difficult birth of a freer society.

Let it be said to the people:

The fight is yours. But fight as builders, not vandals. Fight with vision, not vengeance. Guard what is good. Repair what is broken. And above all, remember: resistance, when joined with love, becomes redemption.

To understand how we have arrived at today's crisis, we must first confront the betrayals of yesterday, not to wallow in guilt but to assume the responsibility that history demands of us. For Haiti to transition from a form of republic to a true republic, we must confront the deeper maladies that have eroded our institutions and weakened our sovereignty.

In the next section, we will examine how internal corruption, foreign intervention, and the erosion of national conscience have steadily undermined the moral and political foundations of the Haitian state. The lesson is not merely historical—it is urgent, contemporary, and deeply ethical. We will not only name the external forces that continue to undermine our republic; we will unmask the habits of mind and heart within our leadership that have allowed these forces to take root and flourish.

Let's start in the next chapter with a brief, informative description of generals Louverture, André Rigaud, and Charles Leclerc. These three pivotal figures played a crucial role in the drama of the Haitian Revolution—the epic struggle for liberty, betrayal, and national birth. From the tragic rivalry between Louverture and Rigaud to the cunning manipulation by Napoleon's envoys, the seeds of our present disorder were sown long ago. Foreign powers learned to exploit our divisions. But worse still, our leaders often opened the door.

PART XI

Corruption, Intervention, and the Erosion of Haitian Sovereignty

CHAPTER 24

The Ghosts of Revolution—Louverture, Rigaud, and Leclerc

They died long ago and yet they are not gone.
Their shadows still walk among us,
whispering lessons we have yet to learn.

—Epigraph by the author

To understand how we arrived at today's crisis, we must revisit the betrayals of yesterday—not to wallow in guilt but to take responsibility for them. If Haiti is to move from being a republic in form to a republic in truth, we must return to the place where the dream was first kindled and where its enemies, both foreign and domestic, first conspired to extinguish it.

The Haitian Revolution was not merely a war for freedom. It was a radical experiment in moral and political transformation: a society of enslaved Africans who dared to proclaim their humanity in defiance of the most powerful empires on Earth. But the revolution also bore within it the seeds of enduring tragedy—divisions of race, class, and vision; ambitions betrayed; and the relentless interference of outside powers.

The lives of three generals—Louverture, Rigaud, and Leclerc—offer more than biographical interest. They illuminate the very patterns that continue to shape our republic's struggle: the battle between unity and ego, liberty and betrayal, sovereignty and subjugation. Let us remember these men not as distant historical figures but as living metaphors for our national conscience.

General Toussaint Louverture (c. 1743–1803): The Liberator Betrayed

Toussaint Louverture was born into slavery on a plantation in the French colony of Saint-Domingue. Though his exact birthdate remains uncertain, his legacy is timeless. Literate, devout, and fiercely intelligent, he became a free man in midlife and studied medicine, Catholicism, and military strategy. When the revolution erupted in 1791, Louverture emerged as its most commanding and visionary leader.

Initially allied with the Spanish, he shifted allegiance to the French Republic in 1794, after the abolition of slavery. As a general, Louverture orchestrated a series of military triumphs against British, Spanish, and counterrevolutionary forces. But he was more than a warrior. He rebuilt the colony's economy, maintained plantations through paid labor, and promoted religious tolerance, order, and meritocracy.

In 1801, he issued a constitution that declared Saint-Domingue autonomous, permanently outlawed slavery, and appointed himself governor for life. For Napoleon, this was intolerable. Leclerc was sent to crush him. Despite his efforts to negotiate peace and protect the gains of the revolution, Louverture was arrested by deceit and deported to France. He died in a freezing prison cell in Fort de Joux in 1803, just months before Haitian independence.

"In overthrowing me, you have only cut down the trunk of the tree of liberty. It will spring up again from the roots, for they are deep and many,"[28] he once said.

His words were prophetic.

General André Rigaud (1761–1811): The Rival of the South

André Rigaud was born in Les Cayes to a White planter and a free Black mother. Sent to France for education, he trained as a military officer. He returned to Saint-Domingue as a respected leader among the free people of color, many of whom owned property and even slaves before the revolution.

Rigaud fought valiantly for the French Republic, helping to expel royalist and foreign forces from the country. However, his vision for Saint-Domingue was shaped by his social class: He sought a society led by the mixed-race elite of the south rather than a full-scale emancipation revolution led by former slaves. This ideological and racial tension eventually set him at odds with Louverture.

The result was civil war: the bitter War of Knives (1799–1800). Though both men claimed loyalty to liberty and the republic, their conflict exposed the fragility of Haitian unity. Louverture's forces, better organized and more populous, defeated Rigaud, who fled to exile in France. He returned briefly during the final struggles for independence but never reclaimed political influence.

---

[28] Toussaint Louverture, quoted in C. L. R. James, *The Black Jacobins: Toussaint L'Ouverture and the San Domingo Revolution* (New York: Vintage International, 1989), 288.

Rigaud's life reminds us that even among revolutionaries, the struggle for power and recognition can fracture a common cause. The wound of this division has never fully healed.

General Charles Leclerc (1772–1802): The Smile of the Empire

Charles Leclerc was a French general and the husband of Pauline Bonaparte, Napoleon's sister. Dashing, ambitious, and trusted by the first consul, Leclerc was dispatched in 1802 to Saint-Domingue at the head of a massive expedition. Officially, his mission was to restore peace and order. In truth, he was sent to break Louverture's power and lay the groundwork for reenslaving the Black population.

At first, Leclerc adopted a diplomatic appearance, even confirming Louverture in his position. But once trust was gained, he moved swiftly. Under false pretenses, he arrested Louverture and shipped him to France. What followed was open rebellion. The people of Saint-Domingue, having experienced liberty, refused to be chained again. Guerrilla warfare intensified. Yellow fever ravaged the French army. And Leclerc, once the proud emissary of the empire, died in the colony he failed to conquer, defeated by both disease and the unbreakable will of a free people.

Their Shadows Remain

The stories of Louverture, Rigaud, and Leclerc are not simply tales of the past. They are eternal echoes in the Haitian conscience. Louverture stands for the disciplined vision of freedom. Rigaud warns of pride and factionalism. Leclerc embodies the seductive cruelty of foreign intervention disguised as aid.

Their lives teach us that a nation's liberty must be guarded not only on battlefields but in its imagination, its unity, and its moral strength. The revolution was won not merely by arms but by the will to be free. That same will must now be called upon again—not to fight the same war but to confront its descendants: corruption, disunity, and external manipulation.

To move forward, Haiti must reckon with its ghosts—not to exorcise them but to learn from them.

CHAPTER 25

From Toussaint Louverture to Today: The Tragic Cost of Division and Foreign Design

Tension is the fire that tests the soul of a people.
To blame the outsider while ignoring the traitor within
is to fight with a blindfold on.
Shatter the divisions, confront the betrayers,
and the world's designs will wither before a united Haiti.

—Epigraph by the author

How does an aspiring nation lose control of its destiny? Not all chains are visible. Not all conquerors march with guns. Sometimes, the failure of people fighting for their freedom begins with whispers of betrayal, bribery, and promises made in smoke-filled rooms. The present Haiti, which is failing, forged in fire and sacrifice, was not merely attacked from without. It has long been sabotaged from within.

The story of Louverture and Rigaud is not merely a chapter in the nation's revolutionary past—it is a mirror reflecting the unresolved tensions of Haitian leadership. What if the greatest threats to our sovereignty have not always worn a foreign flag but have often whispered through our corridors of power? Can a people truly be free if their leaders remain ensnared in the very traps of ambition, division, and shortsightedness that our enemies once laid before us?

Let us descend into this tragic and instructive episode—not to mourn it passively but to wrest from its depths the truths we must confront if Haiti is to rise again.

One of the most tragic and revealing episodes in the country's revolutionary history was the deep rivalry between generals Louverture and Rigaud. This internal conflict, often referred to as the War of Knives, was not merely a personal dispute between two influential individuals. It was a carefully manipulated power struggle, provoked and quietly sustained by the French colonial authorities, designed to divide the revolutionary leadership from within.

As historian Thomas Madiou recounts in *Histoire d'Haïti, Tome 2*, the French government pretended to support the revolutionary leaders while secretly hoping that Toussaint and Rigaud would destroy each other. This strategy of divide and conquer was neither new nor accidental. It was a calculated maneuver. By allowing internal Haitian divisions to fester, particularly the tensions between Black generals and the mulatto elite, the French hoped to weaken all resistance and eventually reestablish slavery throughout the island of Saint-Domingue.

Rigaud refused to submit to the authority of Louverture, despite Louverture's position as the commander in chief. Rigaud controlled the south, where the mulatto elite still held considerable influence, while Louverture, with the support of formerly enslaved Blacks, dominated the north and center. Rather than forging a united front against the looming threat of recolonization, both men allowed their egos, ambitions, and distrust to cloud their judgment. As Madiou observes, many other generals, too, were seduced by personal gain, status, and a desire for autonomy. The result was a civil war. Haitians shed one another's blood while the true enemy—colonial domination—stood in the shadows, waiting. This failure of unity proved fatal.

The French government, under Napoleon, seized the moment. Leclerc was dispatched to Saint-Domingue with an imposing fleet and secret instructions to eliminate Louverture and reimpose slavery. His methods were shrewd. He approached Louverture's loyal generals— notably Christophe—with promises that they would retain their military rank and honors if they sided with the French. Christophe, at first skeptical, was eventually swayed. Many others followed, believing in vain that Leclerc was sincere and would preserve the revolutionary gains.

This manipulation had devastating consequences. After Louverture's surrender, deportation, and death in a French prison, Leclerc and his successor, General Donatien de Rochambeau, revealed their true intentions: massacres, racial terror, and the open reestablishment of slavery. This brutality awakened the dormant unity among the Haitian revolutionary forces. Leaders like Dessalines, Pétion, and Christophe now realized the depth of the French betrayal. They resumed the fight with renewed fury, and by January 1, 1804, Haiti proclaimed its independence—the first Black republic in the world, born from fire, sacrifice, and blood.

And yet, the bitter lesson of division has not been learned.

As Madiou's historical account reminds us, the tragedy of Louverture's downfall was not only caused by French cunning but by a failure of Haitian political consciousness. The desire for personal power, the vanity of rank, and a lack of shared national purpose made it easy for foreign powers to manipulate Haitian leaders then—and sadly, that continues today.

Modern Haiti remains mired in many of the same traps: foreign interference masked as aid, Haitian leaders divided by political ego or ethnic loyalty, and a media all too frequently distracted by ideological infighting rather than focused on the deeper task of raising national consciousness. The lessons of Louverture's betrayal and Christophe's shortsightedness have yet to fully awaken today's political class.

What Haiti needs is not more ideological noise or partisan division but a profound moral and intellectual awakening—a rekindling of patriotic conscience. The Haitian press, civil society, educators, and faith communities must lead the way. They must lift the fog from our history and help leaders and citizens alike see the dangerous patterns repeating themselves.

When leaders sell their integrity for fleeting alliances with powerful outsiders, they do not merely betray themselves—they betray the nation of Haiti. They make the country suffer, handing its future to others who do not love or understand it. This crisis of conscience—this tragic legacy of internal division and foreign manipulation—continues to erode the moral fiber of Haitian leadership.

From Louverture to the present day, the truth remains unchanged: Only a united, conscious, and morally grounded leadership can defend Haiti's sovereignty and fulfill the promise of its revolution. If we forget this truth, if we repeat the errors of the past, then the freedom for which so many died becomes a ghost story fading into memory. But if we remember, if we awaken, then Haiti may yet be reborn—not merely as a republic in name but as a people truly free.

Guardians of the Promise: Haiti's Unfinished Revolution

And so, we are left with a sobering reflection: The fall of Louverture was not solely the triumph of French arms but the failure of Haitian unity. A freedom won with blood was nearly lost to pride, distrust, the enticements of the empire, and the blindness of ambition. The same currents—foreign manipulation, ethnic factionalism, political vanity—continue to swirl in the storm-tossed vessel of modern Haiti.

But this need not be our fate.

We must ask ourselves, with the urgency of a people standing at the edge of history, will we be heirs to the betrayal or guardians of the promise? The tree of liberty that Louverture spoke of still grows, but it is starved for conscience, choked by corruption, and battered by division. It cries out for water from the deep wells of memory, patriotism, and moral clarity.

Let the press become a beacon of truth again. Let our churches, classrooms, and public squares echo with the call to integrity. Let our leaders rise above the lure of foreign approval and partisan gain, and instead plant their feet firmly in the soil of national dignity.

Only then—only when we remember the price of our freedom and the poison of our division—can we hope to complete the revolution Louverture began.

For Haiti was not born to kneel. It was born to rise.

CHAPTER 26

Democracy Betrayed—Foreign Meddling and Internal Decay

What is democracy when ballot boxes are bought,
coffers are looted, and destiny is dictated from abroad?
Betrayal is no accident—it is a design,
crafted by greed and foreign hands.
But the day will come when the betrayed refuse the bargain.

—Epigraph by the author

Why do some nations rise after trauma while others remain caught in a revolving door of despair? How does a people born of the world's first successful slave revolt, deeply rooted in the ideals of liberty, find themselves, again and again, betrayed?

Haiti's democratic journey is a story of resilience shadowed by betrayal. The betrayal of hope by corrupt leaders who enriched themselves while the nation starved. The betrayal of sovereignty by foreign powers, whose "aid" often deepened dependency and disorder. And the betrayal of democracy itself—its name invoked, its spirit ignored.

This chapter confronts those betrayals and the systems that enabled them: chronic corruption, foreign interference, and the erosion of Haitian self-rule. But it also shines a light on the quiet, determined resistance of a people who still dare to hope.

The Machinery of Corruption: When the State Serves Itself

Corruption in Haiti is not a bug in the system—it *is* the system. Since the republic's early days, public office has often been seen not as a sacred trust but as a path to personal gain. The state's resources, from customs revenue to development contracts, have served private fortunes rather than public needs.

One of the most flagrant illustrations of this is the PetroCaribe scandal. Under an agreement with Venezuela, Haiti received subsidized oil, and the billions of dollars in savings were supposed to fund roads, schools, and social programs. Instead, massive sums disappeared. Audits by Haiti's Cour Supérieure des Comptes et du Contentieux Administratif (CSCCA, Haiti's Supreme Audit Institution) revealed layers of mismanagement, embezzlement, and fraudulent contracting that implicated multiple administrations.

But PetroCaribe was only the most visible part of a much larger system. Government payrolls are stuffed with "ghost" employees—those who collect salaries without showing up. Customs officers collaborate in smuggling schemes. Public contracts are routinely awarded not for merit but loyalty. In such a system, the state does not govern; it feeds.

Foreign Meddling and Missionary Politics

No honest account of Haiti's struggle for democracy can ignore the long shadow of foreign interference.

The United States' occupation of Haiti (1915–1934) left lasting scars. American forces rewrote the Constitution, centralized power, disbanded the army, and opened Haiti's land to foreign ownership. It was a conquest in all but name, setting the tone for future interventions under the guise of help.

In the twenty-first century, the baton was passed to the international community. Most notably, the United Nations Stabilization Mission in Haiti (aka MINUSTAH, which stands for *Mission des Nations Unies pour la Stabilisation en Haiti*), a peacekeeping operation deployed from 2004–2017 in the aftermath of political upheaval, was tasked with restoring order and strengthening state institutions. While MINUSTAH brought some security, it also became a source of bitter controversy. Troops were accused of human rights abuses. Infamously, they introduced a cholera epidemic in 2010, a catastrophe that claimed more than ten thousand lives and shattered trust in international missions.

Beyond military presence, foreign governments and global institutions have profoundly shaped Haiti's policy landscape. International NGOs, often bypassing the Haitian state, administer billions in aid. This parallel system of governance, to paraphrase anthropologist Mark Schuller, has undermined local institutions and replaced them with unaccountable technocrats. The effect is paradoxical: aid has poured in, yet state capacity has withered. Policies from security operations to economic strategy are too often dictated in Washington, DC; Geneva, Switzerland; or New York City, New York, rather than in Port-au-Prince.

Economic Dependency and Structural Violence

Haiti's economic chains were forged early. In 1825, France demanded a so-called "independence debt" in exchange for diplomatic recognition. Haiti, just emerging from its revolution, agreed under threat of invasion. The debt, astronomical by any standard, crippled the young nation for over a century.

In more recent times, economic dependency has taken new forms. In the 1980s and 1990s, Haiti came under pressure from the International Monetary Fund and the World Bank to adopt structural adjustment programs, which included tariff reductions, privatization of public enterprises, and austerity measures in social spending. These reforms, while championed as a form of modernization, devastated Haiti's agricultural economy. The country's rice farmers, once self-sufficient, were destroyed by an influx of cheap US rice. Even President Bill Clinton, who supported the policy during his administration, later confessed: "It may have been good for some of my farmers in Arkansas, but it has not worked. It was a mistake."[29]

Medical anthropologist Paul Farmer labeled these consequences *structural violence*—the slow, systemic harm inflicted by policies that deprive people of health, dignity, and livelihood. The pain was not immediate or explosive—it was enduring, invisible, and deeply unjust.

Democratic Forms Without Democratic Substance

Haiti holds elections, but all too frequently they are ceremonial performances, not genuine exercises in democratic choice.

Voter turnout is alarmingly low. Parties are personal vehicles, not policy-driven platforms. Elections are marred by fraud, intimidation, and opaque financing. Many politicians answer more to foreign donors or wealthy patrons than to the people they are meant to represent. Even when elections are funded and monitored by international actors, they rarely

---

[29]Bill Clinton, testimony before the Senate Foreign Relations Committee, March 10, 2010, quoted in "Bill Clinton Apologizes for Past Rice Policies," *Center for Economic and Policy Research*, March 22, 2010.

produce governments that can govern. The emphasis on rapid "stability" over patient institution-building has, ironically, destabilized trust.

In such an environment, democracy becomes a mask worn to appease funders, not to empower citizens. Disillusionment runs deep, and where hope fails, gangs and extralegal power structures fill the void.

Resistance and Reckoning: Voices That Refuse to be Silent

And yet, amid corruption and foreign domination, Haitians have not been silent. Civil society groups such as the Réseau National de Défense des Droits Humains have tirelessly documented abuses and advocated for reform. Investigative journalists, often working under threat, have exposed corruption at the highest levels of government. Human rights lawyers continue to push for accountability, however slow the wheels of justice may turn.

The most iconic recent act of civic awakening came with the PetroCaribe Challenge that young Haitians launched on social media in 2018. Their searing but straightforward question— *"Kot kòb PetroCaribe a?"* ("Where is the PetroCaribe money?")—galvanized a generation. What began as a hashtag evolved into a nationwide protest movement, exposing the rot within the system and refusing to accept the excuses of the past. This is resistance as reckoning—not a flash of outrage but a determined demand for truth.

Reclaiming the Dream of Sovereignty

The road to Haitian democracy is not a matter of starting anew. It is a matter of reclaiming what was stolen: sovereignty, trust, and the revolutionary faith in collective destiny.

To begin, corruption must not only be punished but discredited as a way of life. Foreign aid must support Haitian-led solutions, not replace them. And elections must become more than rituals—they must be rooted in participation, transparency, and justice.

Above all, Haiti must return to the moral clarity of its founding, the belief that liberty is sacred, nonnegotiable, and lived amid struggle. In the words of American philosopher, theologian, and public intellectual Cornel West: "Justice is what love looks like in public."[30]

Let democracy in Haiti be love made visible—a form of justice, dignity, and a people finally rising beyond betrayal.

---

[30]Cornel West, *Race Matters* (Boston: Beacon Press, 1993), 34.

CHAPTER 27

The Sacred Duty of Memory—Media and the Redemption of a People

Consciousness and memory are the quiet architects of history, shaping both the wounds we carry and the redemption we dare to seek.

—Epigraph by the author

What happens to a country when it forgets its own story? What happens when injustice is buried beneath spectacle and suffering is drowned out by noise? Can a people rise if they do not remember why they fell?

In Haiti, these questions strike at the core of the democratic crisis. For decades, the nation has endured betrayal from its leaders, interference from abroad, and a deliberate fog of miseducation and distraction. But the most dangerous betrayal may not be corruption or foreign manipulation—it may be forgetting.

To redeem a wounded democracy, Haiti must remember its past. And no institution is better placed to lead this work of remembrance than the media. Not merely as a reporter but as a moral witness. Not just as an observer but as a guardian of the people's sacred memory. As Holocaust survivor and Nobel laureate Elie Wiesel once said, "To forget the dead would be akin to killing them a second time."[31]

In Haiti, to forget past betrayals is to invite their return.

The Betrayal and the Silence

When public officials lie, steal, and manipulate, they don't just break laws—they break the people's trust. And in Haiti, this betrayal is not an isolated event. It is a system. A republic born in the name of freedom has repeatedly delivered chaos, corruption, and control.

But betrayal alone is not the most significant threat. The greater danger is forgetting who lied. Forgetting what was promised. Forgetting how many times hope was crushed.

This is where the media must rise—not just as a chronicler of facts but as a keeper of collective memory. People who forget their past are more likely to be manipulated into repeating it. When the record is erased, the same corrupt leaders return in new costumes and the chains are forged anew.

Bwa, Bouyon, ak Banbòch: The Politics of Distraction

Haitians have long been aware of the strategy of distraction employed by those in power. It's known by a familiar phrase: *bwa, bouyon, ak banbòch*—the stick, the soup, and the party.

- *Bwa* (the stick) symbolizes coercion—force used to suppress dissent.

---

[31] Elie Wiesel, *Night*, trans. Marion Wiesel (New York: Hill and Wang, 2006), xv.

- *Bouyon* (the soup) represents minimal aid—just enough to survive, never enough to thrive.
- *Banbòch* (the party) is entertainment and distraction—carnivals, music, and festivities that dull the mind and erase memory.

Though Haiti has moved past the most visible forms of state repression, the strategy remains. The baton may no longer be visible, but repression continues—quiet, systemic, and psychological. And *banbòch*, the politics of spectacle, is thriving. Leaders offer music, slogans, and tokens to distract the people from broken promises. Spectacle is a powerful tool of control. As theorist Guy Debord argued in *The Society of the Spectacle*, modern power thrives not on silence but on noise: distracting, disorienting, dazzling.

In such a system, memory is dangerous. It is revolutionary, which is why the media must refuse to be part of the distraction. Instead, it must speak with clarity, conscience, and continuity.

Nou dwe sonje. Nou pa ka bliye.

We must remember. We cannot forget.

Journalism as Ritual and Remembrance

In a wounded republic, journalism must become more than a profession— it must become a moral ritual.

Just as the faithful gather in church to remember suffering and seek guidance, people must turn to their newspapers, radios, and screens for memory and meaning. The media's role is catechetical—to educate, to warn, and to anchor the public in truth.

Democracy is not a gift to be received; it is a gift to be given. It is a responsibility to be embraced. And this responsibility demands education.

An ill-informed public may endure a dictatorship. But in a democracy, ignorance is fatal. It opens the door to manipulation, erodes vigilance, and undermines the integrity of the vote.

Let the press repeat this like a national creed:

You must know. You must watch. You must remember.

Exposing the System, Not Just the Scandal

Too often, the press chases headlines but ignores the deeper currents. The real danger lies not just in the thief but in the system that rewards theft.

The Haitian media must go beyond scandal-driven sensationalism. It must reveal the architecture of corruption: how contracts are awarded, how power is bought, how institutions are hollowed out, and how silence is purchased.

This requires courage. But more than courage, it requires conviction. Every Haitian journalist, broadcaster, and editor must see their work not simply as employment but as a form of resistance. A continuation of Haiti's revolutionary heritage. A stand for truth on behalf of the many who do not know they are being lied to.

Philosopher Hannah Arendt warned that "the ideal subject of totalitarian rule is not the convinced Nazi or [. . .] Communist, but people for whom the distinction between fact and fiction [. . .] no longer exists."[32] The press must safeguard that distinction.

The Call to Moral Awakening

Haiti does not suffer from ignorance alone. It suffers from a moral sleep induced by fear, fatigue, and calculated distractions.

---

[32]Hannah Arendt, *The Origins of Totalitarianism* (New York: Harcourt, Brace & Company, 1951), 474.

The time has come for the Haitian press to lead a moral awakening. This means showing the people how power operates—how elections can be rigged without ever altering a ballot, how foreign aid can prop up failure, how slogans become smoke screens, and how parties are thrown while the republic bleeds.

The media must remind the people of this eternal truth:

Your ancestors did not dance for their liberty. They fought. They sacrificed. They rose in blood and prayer.

Do not trade that legacy for *bouyon* and *banbòch*.

Toward a Media of Sovereignty

Sovereignty is not just territorial—it is spiritual, cultural, and intellectual. The media must help Haiti reclaim this deeper sovereignty. This means producing content in Haitian Creole, not just French. It means telling the stories of heroes and martyrs, not just politicians. It means teaching history, decoding propaganda, and lifting local voices.

Haitian history is not a dry chronicle of dates and decrees. It is an epic of liberty wrested from bondage, of betrayal endured and overcome, of a nation carved from the impossible. It is a tapestry woven with the lives of men and women whose courage defied empires, whose dreams dared to challenge fate. From the volcanic revolution that gave birth to the first Black republic to the turbulent present, Haiti's history is ablaze with stories of resistance, dignity, and national rebirth.

This rich and turbulent past is more than memory—it is a source of strength. It holds within it the moral and civic lessons needed to awaken the nation's sleeping conscience. For the youth so often fed a steady diet of despair, it is a reminder that they are heirs to greatness. For the elders tempted by resignation, it is a summons to perseverance. In this sense, history becomes a sacred flame, not to be enshrined in stone but to be kept alive in people's hearts and homes.

If it awakens to its vocation, the media can become the high priest of this flame. With creativity and purpose, it can reclaim the historical narrative as a tool for national education and moral regeneration. Imagine a well-produced series of televised dramas or documentaries that retell, episode by episode, the saga of the Haitian Revolution: the rise of Louverture, the southern campaigns of Rigaud, the deception of Leclerc, the triumph at Vertières. These are not only compelling tales—they are civic catechisms. The struggle for sovereignty, the cost of disunity, the danger of foreign manipulation, the power of collective will—these themes echo with relevance in every corner of our contemporary life.

Let the media create spaces where the nation remembers through film, radio, podcast, school programs, and theater. Let us no longer allow foreign powers to define our heroes or bury our truths. Instead, let us elevate our narratives, not with bitterness but with boldness and pride. In so doing, the press can fulfill its sacred duty: to redeem the past, guide the future, and remind the people of not only who they were but whom they still might become.

The future of Haiti depends not only on votes but on vision. The press must be the lens that clarifies that vision, raising consciousness, sharpening discernment, and strengthening the people's ability to govern themselves. Ultimately, the media must become a sacred institution—not because it wears robes or incense, but because it carries the weight of the republic's soul.

The Priesthood of Memory

Haiti will not be saved by politicians alone. Donors, elections, or diplomacy will not suffice. It will be saved when the people remember who they are, what they have suffered, and what they must still demand. The media, standing between the people and the palace, between memory and manipulation, must become the new priesthood of the republic.

Not holy in ceremony, but sacred in responsibility.

Not cloaked in ritual, but radiant in truth.

Let its voice remind the people:

Liberty is not a feast. It is a fast, a struggle, a sacred inheritance. Guard it with your life.

PART XII

Reimagining the Republic: Justice, Renewal, and the Media's Covenant

CHAPTER 28

The Path Forward

When we confuse the sky with the weather,
fear turns clouds into prophecy—
and we abandon the work of rebuilding.

—Epigraph by the author

How does a wounded nation heal? Can a people betrayed by leaders, manipulated by foreign powers, and forgotten by the world still shape their destiny on their own terms? Can democracy be reborn, not as an imported ideal but as a living culture—rooted in language, in soil, in spirit?

These are the questions Haiti must face. To speak of hope in Haiti is to speak boldly. It is to resist the narratives of despair, decline, and dependency that have long served the interests of others. But Haiti's story, when told truthfully, is not one of passive suffering. It is a story of resistance, imagination, and sacred endurance.

This chapter is not intended to be a policy manual. It is a vision—a map of what Haiti might become if it rebuilds itself from within, drawing from its own cultural power and historical strength. As philosopher Ernst Bloch suggested, hope is not about predicting the future. It is about preparing for it with imagination and resolve.

Haiti must now ready itself—not for a handout or an intervention, but for a rebirth.

Reclaiming Sovereignty from the Inside Out

Sovereignty is not simply about waving a flag or declaring independence. It is about *agency*—the ability of people to govern themselves with dignity and competence.

For Haiti, true sovereignty begins internally. It means investing in legitimate, local institutions that serve the public good rather than relying on foreign donors or political elites. This includes:

- Strengthening municipal governments and decentralizing decision-making
- Empowering community councils to manage resources and resolve disputes
- Cultivating new generations of ethical, accountable leaders committed to service, not self-enrichment

This internal renewal must be accompanied by nationwide civic education. Haitians must not only know their rights, but also their responsibilities as citizens in a democracy. Sen argues that democracy is not just about institutions but about public reasoning and informed participation. Without civic education, sovereignty becomes a slogan rather than a structure.

Cultivating Civic Culture and Participatory Democracy

Democracy is not a moment. It is a practice.

It lives in everyday interactions—how people deliberate, dissent, and dream together. Haiti must cultivate a democratic culture that extends beyond the ballot box to schools, markets, churches, and homes. This means:

- Revitalizing political parties so they reflect public will, not private ambition
- Protecting civic organizations, neighborhood groups, student unions, and women's movements
- Supporting journalism, education, and the arts as spaces for civic imagination

Democracy must be experienced. A student learning about the Haitian Revolution, a farmer debating land policy at a community meeting, an artist painting Resistance on a city wall—these are the real architects of democratic life. As Freire wrote in *Pedagogy of the Oppressed*, "Education must begin with the solution of the teacher-student contradiction, by reconciling the poles of the contradiction so that both are simultaneously teachers and students." This is what participatory democracy demands: mutual learning and shared power.

Pursuing Justice and Ending Impunity

No nation can move forward when its most powerful citizens are above the law. Haiti cannot build peace without justice, and justice cannot exist in the presence of impunity.

The judiciary must be independent, well resourced, and transparent. Political crimes must not be buried but investigated and brought to a fair trial. Corruption must be confronted, not quietly tolerated.

Truth-telling initiatives such as truth and reconciliation commissions can help acknowledge historical harm while seeking healing, not revenge. Justice must be:

- Restorative, not only punitive
- Accessible, not only to the elite
- Protective, not merely symbolic

South Africa's Truth and Reconciliation Commission showed that nations can move forward only by looking backward honestly and humbly. Haiti, too, must reckon with its past to claim its future.

Building an Inclusive Economy Rooted in Equity

Without economic dignity, political reform is doomed to collapse. A hungry citizen cannot defend democracy. A jobless youth cannot sustain hope.

Haiti's economy must be redesigned to serve all its people, not just its elites. This requires:

- Investing in rural development—supporting small farmers, improving roads, and ensuring food sovereignty
- Encouraging entrepreneurship through microfinance and cooperative models
- Prioritizing public investments in health, education, and housing

Tax reform is essential. Today's system unfairly burdens the poor while shielding the wealthy. A progressive, transparent fiscal policy can reverse this injustice and rebuild public trust. Economist Ha-Joon Chang reminds us that "there is no such thing as a free market." Policy choices shape every economy, and those choices must reflect the moral priorities of justice, not profit.

Reimagining National Identity and Spiritual Renewal

Haiti's wounds are not only material: they are existential. A nation cannot rise if it does not believe in itself.

Haitians must rediscover their history—not just the revolutions and tragedies but the stories of resistance, wisdom, and creativity. The nation's identity must be reimagined through:

- Honoring vodou and other spiritual traditions as sources of moral reflection and resilience
- Celebrating Haitian art, music, storytelling, and ritual as tools of cultural renewal
- Establishing national holidays, museums, and curricula that tell the full, rich story of Haiti's people—not just its emperors and generals but its mothers, poets, teachers, and dreamers

This is about more than memory. It is about meaning.

According to philosopher Kwame Anthony Appiah, a nation's identity is not discovered but crafted—woven from the narratives a people embrace and pass down as their own. Haiti must choose a story of dignity, not despair.

A Covenant with the Future

The road ahead will be long, uncertain, and marked by setbacks. But it must be walked with open eyes, firm feet, and courageous hearts.

Already, the path is being cleared by young organizers in the streets, by farmers returning to their ancestral lands, by teachers refusing to surrender to apathy, by artists painting a new dream on old walls.

To reimagine Haiti is not an act of fantasy—it is an act of faith. A faith in what the nation can still become.

Let this be our collective vow:

Haiti must rise—not by the hand of another but by its sacred strength, not in someone else's image but in its whole truth.

Let the next chapter in Haiti's story be written in the ink of justice, on the parchment of participation, in the language of dignity, and the rhythm of hope.

CHAPTER 29

The Voice of the Covenant—Media as a Bridge to Tomorrow

The future is not fate — it is edited, published, and read.
Each headline is a promise,
each broadcast a blueprint.
Let Haiti's press refuse despair.
Let it turn today's news into tomorrow's justice.

—Epigraph by the author

What do we owe the future?

Can a nation built in blood and resilience still claim a destiny of peace and justice?

And in the face of broken promises and fading dreams, can hope be more than a poetic illusion?

In Haiti, where the struggle for sovereignty has been as fierce as it has been enduring, these questions are not philosophical luxuries. They are daily imperatives. They shape what we build, how we govern, and what we dare to imagine. In this chapter, we ask: what is the role of the media in preparing a just tomorrow? Can journalism help forge a national covenant with the future?

To walk forward with hope, after all, is not naivete—it is courage. It is faith forged in fire.

Covenant with the Future

Haiti's future is not a matter of fate. Still, this vision of the future demands more than the sentiment of fidelity to its founding promise, to the dignity of its people, and to the generations yet unborn who await either the justice we prepare or the ruins we leave behind. It is a moral covenant—a pledge not merely written in constitutions or laws but enacted in daily decisions, elections, and acts of civic responsibility.

In this sacred task, the media must not remain a bystander. It is a covenant-keeper. The press must help write, publish, and uphold this promise, serving as both a prophet of hope and a steward of accountability. In the spirit of Havel, we are reminded that the spoken and written word, anchored in truth, is one of humanity's most enduring and transformative powers. The stories we tell today shape the future our children inherit.

Telling the Future Before It Arrives

The media must not simply report what is—it must illuminate what could be. In a land often flooded with bad news, journalism must become a lantern, not just a mirror.

This section calls for a reimagined purpose of journalism: less reactive, more visionary. Instead of repeating cycles of tragedy, the media should spotlight the people, ideas, and reforms that offer genuine possibility. This includes:

- **Profiles of Courage**

  The young activist in Jacmel forms a civic education club; the grandmother in Gonaïves feeds schoolchildren from her garden; the priest mentors boys so they avoid gang life. These are not sentimental anecdotes—they are the seeds of a better tomorrow. They must be seen, heard, and shared.

- **A Vision Beat**

  A regular section or program that showcases youth visions, local development projects, diaspora initiatives, and technological innovations. Each story should answer the central question: what kind of Haiti are we building?

  As historian Howard Zinn noted, "To be hopeful in bad times is not foolishly romantic. It is based on the fact that human history is a history not only of cruelty, but also of compassion, sacrifice, courage, and kindness."[33] The media must help the public see these stories and believe in them.

Framing Journalism as Generational Stewardship

Every article, every broadcast, and every photograph is not just a record of today. It is a message to the future. Journalism must become intergenerational. It must speak not only for this moment but for the children of tomorrow.

This section advocates for a long-term, ethical approach to media production, centered on responsibility rather than ratings.

To do this:

---

[33]Howard Zinn, "The Optimism of Uncertainty," in *The Impossible Will Take a Little While: A Citizen's Guide to Hope in a Time of Fear*, ed. Paul Rogat Loeb (New York: Basic Books, 2004), 3.

- **Train Journalists to Report with an Eye toward the Future**
  Link today's crises, whether deforestation, corruption, or youth unemployment, to their long-term impacts.

- **Frame Opinion Pieces and Debates with Tomorrow in Mind**
  Ask questions like: if this policy stands, how will it affect the next generation? If this leader governs unchecked, what legacy is being left behind?

This shift from outrage to vigilance cultivates a wiser citizenry—one that is less easily manipulated and more deeply rooted in principle.

Cultivating a Civic Vocabulary for Tomorrow

A democracy grows not only through elections but through language. Words form the building blocks of national consciousness. The media must help construct a civic vocabulary that uplifts, educates, and unites the community.

This section focuses on how language shapes participation. It suggests the media as both a messenger and a moral educator.

- **Launch Campaigns with Hopeful and Inclusive Slogans**
  Nou tout se Ayiti demen. (We are all Haiti tomorrow.)
  Patisipasyon pa se opsyon; se devwa. (Participation is not an option; it is a duty.)

- **Create Children's Media with Democratic Values**
  Programming in Creole—through stories, songs, and ani-

mations—should instill justice, service, and responsibility in children from a young age.

The repetition of civic ideals through media is how a fragmented nation becomes whole.

Protecting the Imagination: Defending the Right to Dream

The right to dream is not written in any law, but it is the foundation of every freedom. When people are robbed of imagination, they are robbed of the future. The press must resist the fatalism that says nothing can change. Yes, it must expose injustice, but without poisoning the well of hope. It must confront reality without crushing the will to act.

This section affirms the media's responsibility to strike a balance between critique and encouragement.

- **Pair Critique with Creativity**

  For every failed project, highlight one that shows promise.

- **Host Public Dialogues**

  Include youth, elders, and civic leaders in televised forums. Let them air both grievances and dreams. Their speech is the soil in which vision grows.

Remember, as Solnit said of hope, "It is an axe you break down doors with in an emergency."[34] In Haiti, the emergency is real—but so is the hope.

---

[34]Rebecca Solnit, *Hope in the Dark: Untold Histories*, Wild Possibilities, 3rd ed. (Chicago: Haymarket Books, 2016), 4–5.

Institutional Memory and Historical Continuity

A covenant with the future requires reverence for the past. People must know where they have been to move wisely toward where they are going. The press must act as both historian and herald.

Historical continuity gives legitimacy to present struggles and fosters collective identity. To that end, the media might:

- **Produce "On This Day in Haitian Democracy" Segments**
  Remind the public of historic speeches, protests, legal milestones, and social victories.

- **Create Accessible Archives**
  Build and preserve documentaries, newspapers, and interviews in Creole, French, and digital formats accessible to students, educators, and communities.

This practice of remembrance arms citizens with perspective and pride.

A Watchdog for the Children

Ultimately, the covenant with the future is about one thing: *accountability to the unborn*.

Every shuttered school, every stolen dollar, every uninvestigated abuse is a debt paid by the next generation. The press must be their advocate and defender.

This section redefines the watchdog role of the media in long-term moral terms—not merely exposing corruption but protecting posterity.

It must ask:

- Is this decision sustainable?
- Will this law nourish or starve tomorrow's citizens?
- Are we preparing young people to lead or leaving them to clean up our mistakes?

These are the questions of a mature media—a press worthy of its power.

The Press as Witness and Architect

To help write a covenant with the future is to believe that today is not the end of the story. It is to speak for the unborn, for the dignity of the living, and for the justice of those long gone. In this sacred task, the media must be both witness and architect, faithfully recording history and boldly shaping it.

Let it be said that in Haiti's darkest hours, the press did not surrender to despair, spectacle, or silence. It chose instead to keep the lamp of truth burning, to give voice to hope, and to defend the dream of a sovereign and human nation.

For the ancestors who died.

For the children who will rise.

This is the media's vow. This is its sacred task.

We can close this chapter by returning to the guiding line at the end of chapter 22: Haiti's media should not be the echo of other countries. It should be the echo of its own voice, resonating with the cadence of its history and the timbre of its struggle. The press must be tailored to Haiti's specific challenges, for in that authenticity lies the solution to the Haitian struggle.

CHAPTER 30

Rewriting the Code: Toward a Republic of Conscience

Nations do not rise by decree.
They rise when the code of conscience is rewritten—
when law, memory, and the soul of a people learn to speak the same
truth.

Epigraph by the author

What makes a nation rise—or fall?
Is it laws and elections alone, or something deeper? Something written not just in statutes but in the spirit of the people?

In Haiti, the search for democracy cannot be separated from the question of identity. What kind of people are we shaping? What values are we passing on to the next generation? What vision do we hold for our future?

This chapter asks not only what Haiti must change in its politics but what it must transform in its soul. To move toward a stable democracy, Haiti must rewrite the hidden code that shapes public life: the moral habits, cultural patterns, and civic imagination of its people. That work begins with vision, but it depends on education, media, and the cultivation of character.

The Open Future: Crisis and Possibility

The future of Haiti is not sealed by fate. It remains open and uncertain, yes, but filled with sacred potential. This book has traced the contours of Haiti's crises: political instability, corruption, violence, and the spiritual struggle for meaning. Yet it has also testified to something more enduring: the unbreakable will of the Haitian people. Their creativity, resilience, memory, and hunger for justice speak louder than any despair. The question now is not whether change is possible; it is whether it is feasible. It is whether we have the courage—moral, intellectual, and civic—to build it.

Rewriting the Code of Public Life

To rebuild Haitian democracy is to *rewrite the code* that underlies it. Not just in government but in the deeper patterns of how society thinks, feels, and acts. For too long, Haiti's civic institutions have been corrupted by forces such as cynicism, greed, betrayal, and the misuse of culture for political gain. The code here is a metaphor for the invisible habits and narratives that shape national behavior, much like software determines how a system functions.

When these forces repeat over generations, they form a dark pattern that regenerates poverty, fear, and hopelessness. If Haiti is to move toward a republic of dignity and self-rule, this pattern must be broken. The code must be rewritten.

That begins with vision: a moral and practical blueprint for national renewal. But vision alone is not enough. It must be reinforced through repetition—a steady rhythm of habits, values, and symbols practiced daily in homes, schools, media, and public life.

The Media as Moral Architect

In this sacred effort, the media must step beyond its role as mere observer or entertainer. It must become a *moral architect*, a teacher of conscience. Instead of chasing spectacle, it must spotlight substance. Instead of echoing chaos, it must amplify clarity.

This is a call to reform journalism—not only in its content but in its function. Media must help build shared understanding, not just report fragmentation. The press must draw from Haiti's cultural wellspring, including the metaphorical and spiritual language of vodou, to translate complex truths into messages that move the heart and awaken the civic spirit. Media must not only inform but also inspire.

As Freire once wrote: "Liberating education consists in acts of cognition, not transferals of information."[35] In the same way, liberating journalism must awaken understanding, not just deliver headlines.

The Classroom as Civic Sanctuary

Schools must also be rebuilt—not just with bricks but with soul. Haitian classrooms must become spaces of thought, dialogue, and moral formation. They must not merely train students to survive but to serve, lead, and think. At the center of this effort lies the formation of what psychologists and anthropologists call the basic personality: the deep-set traits, values,

---

[35]Paulo Freire, *Pedagogy of the Oppressed*, trans. Myra Bergman Ramos (New York: Continuum, 1970), 79.

and behaviors shared across a culture.

Understanding Basic Personality

Basic personality refers to the mental and emotional framework that people internalize as members of a society. It shapes how individuals think, feel, and act, reflecting the shared "style" of a culture. As anthropologist Ralph Linton observed, this helps explain why the Comanche act like Comanche or the French like French. It's what gives a culture coherence and continuity.

Think of basic personality as the invisible mold into which a society casts its citizens. It doesn't dictate everything, but it forms the base.

This personality is not inborn; four key factors shape it:

- Hereditary factors, such as family customs and inherited tendencies
- Social factors, including institutions, norms, and relationships
- Environmental factors, such as geography and physical surroundings
- Emotional factors, such as experiences of fear, joy, loss, and belonging

Each of these interacts to form a person's core sense of self, deeply tied to their cultural context.

Culture and Integration

Linguist Edward Sapir defined cultural elements as learned behaviors or symbols passed down through society, like hunting techniques, poems, religious objects, or political rituals. These elements aren't biological; they are social and symbolic. And they help form the basic personality.

Culture isn't just music or dress. It's how people assign meaning to life and how that meaning is passed down across generations. When basic personality incorporates these cultural symbols, it expresses the soul of a people.

The Risk of Fragmentation

But what happens when a society contains multiple, competing cultural systems?

In Haiti, this is a lived reality. On one hand, there is a cultural world associated with the educated elite that is fluent in French and shaped by Western institutions. On the other hand, there is the deeply rooted cultural universe of the popular masses that is grounded in Haitian Creole and vodou traditions, and often distanced from formal education. While both groups reside in the same nation, they often inhabit different symbolic worlds. As a result, many Haitian children grow up between these worlds, unsure of where they belong. Their basic personality is stretched between competing norms, and sometimes, it does not fully form in either system. This can lead to confusion, contradiction, and emotional vulnerability.

The Role of Institutions

To prevent such fragmentation, schools, media, and civic organizations must intervene. Their task is to build a cultural bridge, helping young people form a coherent identity that honors Haiti's diversity while pointing toward a shared national vision.

The long-term health of any society depends on whether its institutions transmit unity or division. This means teaching not just reading and writing but also how to *choose, question,* and *care.* Students must learn their rights and responsibilities to themselves, their community, and future generations.

The Crisis Is Moral

Haiti does not lack spirit. It lacks *vision*. It suffers from a crisis of moral instruction—a breakdown in the shared story of what it means to be a citizen, a neighbor, a Haitian.

To heal this fracture, education and media must form a partnership. Their shared mission is nothing less than civilizational renewal to awaken the intellect and the civic soul.

Leadership as Equilibrium

In classical mechanics, equilibrium is achieved by balancing opposing forces with the proper supports. The same principle applies to society. Leadership must serve as a moral fulcrum, balancing tensions without collapse.

- The president must lead not as a ruler, but as a steadying force.
- The press must shine light, not pour fuel.
- The school must cultivate citizens, not passive test-takers.

And the people themselves, especially the Haitian masses, must believe in their agency. Power alone is not enough. It must be joined with discernment, knowledge, and purpose.

A Covenant with the Future

Let this then be our covenant:

We will no longer live under the tyranny of forgetfulness.

The media will serve not as spectacle but truth.

The school will raise not only graduates, but guardians of the republic.

Politics will be reclaimed, not by gangs or opportunists but by citizens who care.

And that Haiti, the first among Black republics, will rise again.

Not by magic.

Not by foreign pity.

But through the slow, luminous labor of moral renewal.

This is no small task. It is the work of generations.

But it is the only work worthy of a nation born in fire, baptized in struggle, and destined for liberty.

Society is more than just a collection of individuals. As Émile Durkheim said, it forms a distinct reality shaped by the relationships and structures that bind people to one another. Let us build that reality together—a republic of conscience.

Let the code be rewritten.

Let the republic be reborn.

Memory, Consciousness, and the Rebirth of Haiti

We were not born to bow before the blows of fate.
We were born to strike the sacred drum of destiny
and call forth a future worthy of our name.

—Epigraph by the author

Whatdoes it take for a nation to heal?
Can a country fractured by violence and injustice ever become whole again? And what role do memory, responsibility, and spirit play in the long, uncertain path toward democracy?

These are not abstract questions for Haiti. They are the urgent riddles of a wounded nation that refuses to die. In the face of chaos and despair, the Haitian people continue to rise with resilience, faith, and a deep hunger for dignity.

This afterword does not offer easy answers. Instead, it presents a more profound reckoning—a vision of Haiti's future that depends not just on politics or policy but on something more profound: the rebirth of national consciousness.

Beyond Reform: The Need for Moral Awakening

As we reach the end of this journey through Haiti's tangled crises—of politics and power, gangs and gods, democracy betrayed and humanity wounded—one truth emerges clearly: No constitutional rewrite, no quick election, no international summit can redeem the republic on its own. Real change cannot come from the surface alone. It must rise from the depths of the Haitian soul.

What Haiti needs is a moral awakening—a transformation that touches not just laws but lives. A return to conscience. A resurrection of the spirit.

This sets the stage for a deeper vision of reform, one rooted in the moral and cultural life of the people, not just in statecraft.

This book has presented many hard truths about the erosion of public institutions, the failures of the press, the manipulation of faith, and the prolonged silence of justice. But beneath those specifics lies a larger question: how does a people long battered by history reclaim their dignity and reshape their destiny?

The Three Pillars of Renewal: Experience, Understanding, and Remembrance

True national renewal rests on three timeless pillars: experience, understanding, and remembrance.

Every person endures hardship. And Haiti has walked through fire, from revolution to occupation, from dictatorship to gang rule. These experiences are not just wounds; they are lessons. But lessons must be understood.

Experience alone doesn't shape maturity—reflection does. This section connects personal and collective growth to historical consciousness.

It is not enough to suffer. The suffering must be made intelligible, examined, reflected upon, and turned into wisdom. And even wisdom fades unless it is remembered—preserved through stories, rituals, and civic life.

Haiti's history lives in blood and prayer, in drums and resistance. But without reflection, pain remains trauma. And without memory, there is no learning—only repetition. As philosopher George Santayana warned: "Those who cannot remember the past are condemned to repeat it."[36]

So it is with nations. If Haiti forgets her past, she risks losing her future—not through war but through amnesia.

Memory as Civic Foundation

To remember, in this context, is not to dwell in sorrow. It is to guard the soul of the nation.

Memory is not nostalgia—it is civic responsibility. It provides the foundation upon which a people can build justice. And it offers a mirror that reflects both failure and promise. This invites the reader to consider memory as a collective moral compass, not just a repository of historical knowledge.

Haiti's educators, journalists, artists, and leaders all share in this responsibility. They are the keepers of the national memory. If they fail, democracy withers in barren soil.

---

[36]George Santayana, *The Life of Reason: Or the Phases of Human Progress*, vol. 1, *Reason in Common Sense* (New York: Charles Scribner's Sons, 1905), 284.

But if memory is cultivated with reverence and clarity, a new Haiti can take root. A nation that knows itself cannot be easily broken.

Consciousness and Responsibility: The Soul of the Nation

Haiti's current crisis is not divine punishment, nor a random accident. It is a consequence—shaped by colonial trauma, foreign interference, yes, but also by our reactions to adversity.

This section begins a crucial shift from blame to accountability. It honors external injustices without ignoring internal responsibilities. For every chain imposed from outside, there are shackles we have fastened ourselves: apathy, corruption, fatalism, and indifference to reform.

We must hold up the mirror not just to empires, but to ourselves as well. As James Baldwin once wrote, "Not everything that is faced can be changed. But nothing can be changed until it is faced."[37]

True consciousness is not just awareness. It is a moral awakening. It is the courage to ask:

- How do we interpret our suffering?
- What do we teach our children?
- What future are we building, one small decision at a time?

If we meet hardship with resignation, decay follows. But if we face it with clear-eyed determination and fidelity to justice, we awaken something powerful: a redemptive force no empire can destroy.

---

[37]James Baldwin, "As Much Truth As One Can Bear," *New York Times Book Review,* January 14, 1962, 1.

The Power of Collective Consciousness

Until the Haitian people become fully conscious of their story—its pain, its courage, and its contradictions—they cannot learn. And without learning, there can be no remembrance. Without remembrance, there is no future.

To celebrate 1804 every year is not enough. Pride without reflection becomes arrogance. Victory without vigilance becomes myth.

Democracy is not a gift. It is a daily covenant—renewed by conscious, courageous citizens who demand truth, protect justice, and carry the dream forward. This emphasizes that the responsibility of democracy is shared. It is a lived practice, not a distant ideal.

That task belongs to everyone: students, merchants, mothers, musicians, clergy, journalists, and the diaspora. All must take up the work. All must live not just for survival but for significance.

To live unconsciously is to wither. To live with conscience is to build something lasting—something worthy of our children and of history itself.

A Prayer for the Rising

To write about Haiti is to stand at the edge of both sorrow and strength.

It is to witness a people who have endured the worst yet still believe in the best. A land where gods walk with the wounded and where every drumbeat is a call to remember, resist, and rebuild.

This book is not an ending. It is an invocation—a call to action, not only for leaders and scholars but for every Haitian to rise to the sacred labor of building a just and sovereign nation.

Democracy cannot be imported. It cannot be imposed. It must be sung into being—in Creole and protest, in prayer and policy, in song and service. It must be nurtured like a child: with patience, love, and unwavering resolve.

Let this be our vow:

Haiti shall not be defined by what was done to her, but by what she dares to become.

Closing Reflection

What lies ahead for Haiti is not guaranteed. But neither is it lost.

The power to change course—the power to renew and rebuild—rests in the memory, the consciousness, and the will of her people. If that power is awakened, no obstacle is insurmountable. And if it is ignored, no reform will ever be enough.

So let us choose to remember. Let us live with responsibility. Let us act with conscience. For the rebirth of Haiti depends not on fate, but on us.

REFERENCES

Abbott, Elizabeth. *Haiti: The Duvaliers and Their Legacy.* New York: McGraw-Hill, 1988.

Anderson, Benedict. *Imagined Communities: Reflections on the Origin and Spread of Nationalism.* Rev. ed. London: Verso, 2006.

Appiah, Kwame Anthony. *The Ethics of Identity.* Princeton, NJ: Princeton University Press, 2005.

———. *The Lies That Bind: Rethinking Identity.* New York: Liveright, 2018.

Arendt, Hannah. *The Origins of Totalitarianism.* New York: Harcourt Brace & Co., 1951.

Barber, Benjamin. *Strong Democracy: Participatory Politics for a New Age.* Berkeley: University of California Press, 1984.

Bell, Madison Smartt. *Toussaint Louverture: A Biography.* New York: Pantheon Books, 2007.

Bellegarde-Smith, Patrick. *Haitian Vodou: Spirit, Myth, and Reality.* Bloomington: Indiana University Press, 2006.

Benedict, Ruth. *Patterns of Culture.* Boston, MA: Houghton Mifflin, 1934.

Berlin, Isaiah. *Two Concepts of Liberty.* Oxford, England: Clarendon Press, 1958.

Bloch, Ernst. *The Principle of Hope*. Translated by Neville Plaice, Stephen Plaice, and Paul Knight. Cambridge, MA: MIT Press, 1986.

Boff, Leonardo. *Church: Charism and Power: Liberation Theology and the Institutional Church*. Translated by John W. Diercksmeier. New York: Crossroad, 1985.

Bourdieu, Pierre. *Outline of a Theory of Practice*. Cambridge, MA: Cambridge University Press, 1977.

Brown, Karen McCarthy. *Mama Lola: A Vodou Priestess in Brooklyn*. Berkeley: University of California Press, 2011.

Casimir, Jean. *The Haitians: A Decolonial History*. Chapel Hill: University of North Carolina Press, 2020.

Castor, Suzy. "Democracy and Society in Haiti: Structures of Domination and Resistance to Change." In *Latin America Faces the Twenty-First Century*. Edited by Susanne Jonas and Edward McCaughan. Translated by Miriam Ellis. San Francisco, CA: Westview Press, 1994.

Chang, Ha-Joon. *23 Things They Don't Tell You About Capitalism*. New York: Bloomsbury Press, 2010.

Chambers, Frances. *Haiti*. 2nd rev. and expanded ed. World Bibliographical Series, vol. 39. Santa Barbara, CA: Clio Press, 1999.

Chomsky, Noam, Paul Farmer, and Amy Goodman. *Getting Haiti Right This Time: The U.S. and the Coup*. Monroe, ME: Common Courage Press, 2004.

Clinton, William J. Testimony before the Senate Foreign Relations Committee on Haiti. March 10, 2010. United States Senate. https://www.foreign.senate.gov/hearings/rebuilding-haiti-031010.

Collier, David. *The New Authoritarianism in Latin America*. Princeton, NJ: Princeton University Press, 1979.

Cour Supérieure des Comptes et du Contentieux Administratif (CSCCA). *Rapport d'audit spécifique de gestion du Fonds PetroCaribe, Rapport 1.* Port-au-Prince: CSCCA, January 31, 2019. https://cscca.gouv.ht/uploads/documents/1748211406_petrocaribe_rapport_1_31_janv_2019l.pdf

Dahl, Robert. *Democracy and Its Critics.* New Haven, CT: Yale University Press, 1989.

———. *Polyarchy: Participation and Opposition.* New Haven, CT: Yale University Press, 1971.

Dalmas, M. *Histoire de la Révolution de Saint-Domingue, depuis le commencement des troubles jusqu'à la prise de Jérémie et du Môle Saint-Nicolas par les Anglais; suivie d'un mémoire sur le rétablissement de cette colonie.* Tome premier. Paris: Mame Frères, 1814.

Debord, Guy. *The Society of the Spectacle.* Translated by Donald Nicholson-Smith. New York: Zone Books, 1994.

"Declaration of the Rights of Man and of the Citizen, 1789." In *The French Revolution and Human Rights: A Brief Documentary History.* Edited and translated by Lynn Hunt. Boston: Bedford/Saint Martin's Press, 1996.

Dewey, John. *Democracy and Education: An Introduction to the Philosophy of Education.* New York: Macmillan, 1916.

Dorsainvil, J. C. *Vodou et névrose.* Port-au-Prince: Imprimerie de l'État, 1940.

———. *Psychologie haïtienne: Vodou et magie.* Port-au-Prince: Imprimerie de l'État, 1936.

———. *Manuel d'histoire d'Haïti. Avec la collaboration des Frères de l'Instruction.* Port-au-Prince: Chrétienne, 1925.

Dubois, Laurent. *Haiti: The Aftershocks of History.* New York: Metropolitan Books, 2012.

———. *Avengers of the New World: The Story of the Haitian Revolution.* Cambridge, MA: Harvard University Press, 2004.

Dufrenne, Mikel. *La personnalité de base: Un concept sociologique.* Bibliothèque de sociologie contemporaine. Paris: Presses Universitaires de France, 1953.

Dupuy, Alex. *Haiti: From Revolutionary Slaves to Powerless Citizens: Essays on the Politics and Economics of Underdevelopment, 1804–2013.* New York: Routledge, 2014.

———. *Haiti in the New World Order: The Limits of the Democratic Revolution.* Boulder, CO: Westview Press, 1997.

———. *Haiti in the World Economy: Class, Race, and Underdevelopment Since 1700.* Boulder, CO: Westview Press, 1989.

———. *The Prophet and Power: Jean-Bertrand Aristide, the International Community, and Haiti.* Lanham, MD: Rowman & Littlefield, 2007.

Durkheim, Émile. *Les formes élémentaires de la vie religieuse.* Paris: Félix Alcan, 1912.

———. *The Division of Labor in Society.* Translated by W. D. Halls. New York: Free Press, 1997.

———. *The Rules of Sociological Method.* Translated by W. D. Halls. New York: Free Press, 1982. Originally published 1895.

"Election Soup Leaves a Big Mess." *This Week in Haiti,* June 28–July 4, 1995.

Erikson, Daniel P. "The Haiti Dilemma." *Brown Journal of World Affairs* 12, no. 1 (2005): 181–190.

Evans-Smith, William, ed. *Haiti: A Country Study*. 4th ed. Washington, DC: The American University, Foreign Area Studies, 1989.

Fanon, Frantz. *The Wretched of the Earth*. Translated by Richard Philcox. New York: Grove Press, 2004.

Farmer, Paul. *Pathologies of Power: Health, Human Rights, and the New War on the Poor*. Berkeley: University of California Press, 2003.

———. *The Uses of Haiti*. 3rd ed. Monroe, ME: Common Courage Press, 2006.

Fatton Jr., Robert. *Haiti's Predatory Republic: The Unending Transition to Democracy*. Boulder, CO: Lynne Rienner Publishers, 2002.

———. *The Roots of Haitian Despotism*. Boulder, CO: Lynne Rienner Publishers, 2007.

Faulkner, William. *Requiem for a Nun*. New York: Random House, 1951.

"Fear Swarms Around Haiti." *Daily News*. January 3, 1999.

Ferguson, James. *Papa Doc, Baby Doc: Haiti and the Duvaliers*. Oxford, England: Blackwell, 1987.

Fick, Carolyn E. *The Making of Haiti: The Saint Domingue Revolution from Below*. Knoxville: University of Tennessee Press, 1990.

Fitzgibbon, Russell H. and Julio A. Fernandez. *Latin America: Political Culture and Development*. Englewood Cliffs, NJ: Prentice-Hall, 1981.

François, Pierre. *Les Forces armées d'Haïti: Entre pouvoir, discipline, et déroute*. Port-au-Prince: Éditions de l'Université d'État d'Haïti, 2013.

Freire, Paolo. *Pedagogy of the Oppressed*. 30th Anniversary ed. Translated by Myra Bergman Ramos. New York: Continuum, 2000.

Fromm, Erich. *The Sane Society*. New York: Rinehart, 1955.

Gage, Thomas. *The Military in Haitian Politics: A Historical Overview.* Port-au-Prince: Centre de Documentation Haïtienne, 1994.

Geertz, Clifford. *The Interpretation of Cultures.* New York: Basic Books, 1973.

Gros, Jean Germain. "Haiti's Flagging Transition." *Journal of Democracy* 8, no. 4 (1997): 94–97.

"Haiti's Former Leader Jean-Claude Duvalier Dies." *BBC News.* October 4, 2014. https://www.bbc.com/news/world-latin-america-29493785.

Hall, Stuart. "Cultural Identity and Diaspora." In *Colonial Discourse and Post-Colonial Theory: A Reader.* Edited by Patrick Williams and Laura Chrisman, 392–403. New York: Columbia University Press, 1994.

Hallward, Peter. *Damming the Flood: Haiti, Aristide, and the Politics of Containment.* London: Verso, 2007.

Havel, Václav. *Disturbing the Peace: A Conversation with Karel Hvížďala.* Translated by Paul Wilson. New York: Alfred A. Knopf, 1990.

———. *Living in Truth: Twenty-Two Essays Published on the Occasion of the Award of the Erasmus Prize to Václav Havel.* Edited by Jan Vladislav. London: Faber & Faber, 1989.

Hayek, Friedrich A. *The Constitution of Liberty.* Chicago: University of Chicago Press, 1960.

Heinl, Robert Debs, and Nancy Gordon Heinl. *Written in Blood: The Story of the Haitian People, 1492–1995.* Rev. ed. Lanham, MD: University Press of America, 2005.

Hite, Katherine Juliet Roberts. "Problematizing Authoritarian Legacies and Good Democracy." Paper presented at the Maxwell School of Citizenship and Public Affairs, Syracuse University, fall 1999.

Human Rights Watch. *"Haiti: Human Rights Developments."* In *World Report 1999*. https://www.hrw.org/world-report/1999/country-chapters/haiti.

Hunt, Lynn, ed. *The French Revolution and Human Rights: A Brief Documentary History*. Boston: Bedford/Saint Martin's Press, 1996.

Inkeles, Alex. "Totalitarianism and Ideologies." In *Totalitarianism*. Edited by Carl J. Friedrich. Cambridge: Harvard University Press, 1954.

International Crisis Group. *Combating Gang Violence in Haiti*. Brussels: International Crisis Group, 2023.

———. *Controlling Haiti's Gang Violence*. Brussels: International Crisis Group, 2021.

———. *"Haiti: A Path to Stability for a Nation in Crisis."* *Latin America & Caribbean Report* no. 91. Brussels: International Crisis Group, 2021. https://www.crisisgroup.org/latin-america-caribbean/haiti/91-haiti-path-stability-nation-crisis.

James, C. L. R. *The Black Jacobins: Toussaint L'Ouverture and the San Domingo Revolution*. 2nd ed. New York: Vintage, 1989.

Karl, Terry Lynn. "Dilemmas of Democratization in Latin America." Course reader. Latin American Politics, Syracuse University, all 1998.

Kolbe, Athena, and Robert Muggah. "Haiti's Urban Crime Wave." *Foreign Affairs*, February 14, 2012. https://www.foreignaffairs.com/articles/haiti/2012-02-14/haitis-urban-crime-wave.

Lawyers Committee for International Human Rights. *Violations of Human Rights in Haiti*. June 1981; September 1982; June 1984.

Lecomte du Noüy, Pierre. *Human Destiny*. New York: Longmans, Green and Co., 1947.

Le Nouvelliste. Various interviews with former gang members. Port-au-Prince: Le Nouvelliste, 2021. https://lenouvelliste.com.

Lévi-Strauss, Claude. *The Savage Mind.* Chicago: University of Chicago Press, 1966.

Linz, J. Juan. "An Authoritarian Regime: Spain." In *Cleavages, Ideologies, and Party Systems.* Edited by Erik Allardt and Yrjö Littunen. Helsinki: Westermarck Society, 1964.

Linz, J. Juan, and Alfred Stepan. *Problems of Democratic Transition and Consolidation: Southern Europe, South America, and Post-Communist Europe.* Baltimore: Johns Hopkins University Press, 1996.

Locke, John. *Two Treatises of Government.* Edited by Peter Laslett. Cambridge, MA: Cambridge University Press, 1988.

Madiou, Thomas. *Histoire d'Haïti: Tome II, de 1799 à 1803.* Port-au-Prince: Éditions Henri Deschamps, 1989.

———. *Histoire d'Haïti: Tome III, de 1804 à 1806.* Port-au-Prince: Éditions Henri Deschamps, 1989.

Magna Carta. 1215. In *English Historical Documents.* Edited by David C. Douglas, vol. 2, 1042–1189. London: Eyre & Spottiswoode, 1953.

Mainwaring, Scott, and Timothy Scully, eds. *Building Democratic Institutions: Party Systems in Latin America.* Stanford, CA: Stanford University Press, 1995.

McAlister, Elizabeth. *Rara! Vodou, Power, and Performance in Haiti and Its Diaspora.* Berkeley: University of California Press, 2002.

Mead, Margaret. *Coming of Age in Samoa: A Psychological Study of Primitive Youth for Western Civilization.* New York: William Morrow, 1928.

Mintz, Sidney W. *Caribbean Transformations*. Chicago: Aldine, 1974.

Montesquieu, Charles-Louis de Secondat. *Extraits de l'esprit des lois et des oeuvres diverses*. Edited by Camille Julian. Paris: Librairie Hachette, 1901.

Nicholls, David. *From Dessalines to Duvalier: Race, Colour and National Independence in Haiti*. New Brunswick, NJ: Rutgers University Press, 1996.

Niebuhr, Reinhold. *The Irony of American History*. Chicago: University of Chicago Press, 2008.

O'Neill, William G., and Elliot J. Schrage. *Paper Laws, Still Bayonets: Breakdown of the Rule of Law in Haiti*. New York: Lawyers Committee for Human Rights, 1990. http://www.hartford-hwp. com/archives/43a/117.html.

Peeler, John. *Building Democracy in Latin America*. Boulder, CO: Lynne Rienner Publishers, 1998.

Price-Mars, Jean. *Ainsi parla l'Oncle*. Paris: Imprimerie de Compiègne, 1928.

Przeworski, Adam. *Democracy and the Market: Political and Economic Reforms in Eastern Europe and Latin America*. New York: Cambridge University Press, 1991.

Ramsey, Kate. *The Spirits and the Law: Vodou and Power in Haiti*. Chicago: University of Chicago Press, 2011.

Raynal, Guillaume-Thomas. *Histoire philosophique et politique des établissements et du commerce des Européens dans les deux Indes*. Geneva: Jean-Léonard Pellet, 1770.

Réseau National de Défense des Droits Humains. *Rapport sur les exactions perpétrées par les groupes armés dans la zone métropolitaine*. Port-au-Prince: RNDDH, 2021. https://web.rnddh.org.

Sapir, Edward. *Culture, Language and Personality: Selected Essays*. Edited by David G. Mandelbaum. Berkeley: University of California Press, 1949.

Sen, Amartya. *Development as Freedom*. New York: Alfred A. Knopf, 1999.

———. *The Idea of Justice*. Cambridge, MA: Belknap Press of Harvard University Press, 2009.

Schuller, Mark. *Humanitarian Aftershocks in Haiti*. New Brunswick, NJ: Rutgers University Press, 2016.

———. *Killing With Kindness: Haiti, International Aid, and NGOs*. New Brunswick, NJ: Rutgers University Press, 2012.

Schuller, Mark, and Pablo Morales, eds. *Tectonic Shifts: Haiti Since the Earthquake*. Sterling, VA: Kumarian Press, 2012.

Schumpeter, Joseph A. *Capitalism, Socialism, and Democracy*. 3rd ed. New York: Harper & Bros., 1950.

Scott, James C. *Domination and the Arts of Resistance: Hidden Transcripts*. New Haven: Yale University Press, 1990.

Smith, Jennie M. "René Préval and the Return of Lavalas." In *Haiti: Hope for a Fragile State*. Edited by Yasmine Shamsie and Andrew S. Thompson, 65–83. Waterloo, ON: Wilfrid Laurier University Press, 2006.

Smith, Matthew J. *Red & Black in Haiti: Radicalism, Conflict, and Political Change, 1934–1957*. Chapel Hill: University of North Carolina Press, 2009.

Solnit, Rebecca. *Hope in the Dark: Untold Histories, Wild Possibilities*. Chicago: Haymarket Books, 2016.

Sprague, Jeb. *Paramilitarism and the Assault on Democracy in Haiti*. New York: Monthly Review Press, 2012.

Steiner, Henry J., and Philip Alston. *International Human Rights in Context*. Oxford, England: Clarendon Press, 1996.

Taylor, Charles. *Sources of the Self: The Making of the Modern Identity*. Cambridge, MA: Harvard University Press, 1989.

———. *The Malaise of Modernity*. Toronto: House of Anansi, 1991.

"The Worst Is Yet to Come." *Haiti Observateur*. December 15–22, 1999.

Trouillot, Michel-Rolph. *Haiti: State Against Nation*. New York: Monthly Review Press, 1990.

———. *Silencing the Past: Power and the Production of History*. Boston: Beacon Press, 1995.

Ulysse, Gina Athena. *Why Haiti Needs New Narratives: A Post-Quake Chronicle*. Middletown, CT: Wesleyan University Press, 2015.

United Nations. "MINUSTAH: United Nations Stabilization Mission in Haiti." https://peacekeeping.un.org/en/mission/past/minustah/.

United Nations Commission on Human Rights. *Situation of Human Rights in Haiti*. Resolution 1997/52, 53rd session, April 15, 1997. UN Doc. E/CN.4/RES/1997/52. http://www.unhchr.ch/html/menu4/chrres/1997.res/52.html.

United Nations Security Council. *Report of the Secretary-General on Haiti*. New York: United Nations, April 2004.

United States. *The Constitution of the United States of America: With the Declaration of Independence and the Bill of Rights*. Washington, DC: United States Government Publishing Office, 2009.

US Department of State. *Haiti Human Rights Practices*. 1994–1998. Gopher links (archived).

Vygotsky, Lev S. *Mind in Society: The Development of Higher Psychological Processes*. Cambridge, MA: Harvard University Press, 1978.

Weber, Max. "Politics as a Vocation." In *From Max Weber: Essays in Sociology*. Translated by H. H. Gerth and C. Wright Mills, 77–128. New York: Oxford University Press, 1946.

Weil, Thomas E., et al. *Haiti: A Country Study*. Washington, DC: Library of Congress, 1973.

West, Cornel. *Democracy Matters: Winning the Fight Against Imperialism*. New York: Penguin Press, 2004.

Wiesel, Elie. *Night*. Translated by Marion Wiesel. New York: Hill and Wang, 2006.

Wilentz, Amy. *Farewell, Fred Voodoo: A Letter from Haiti*. New York: Simon & Schuster, 2013.

World Bank. *Haiti: Options and Opportunities for Inclusive Growth*. Washington, DC: World Bank Publications, 2015.

ACKNOWLEDGMENTS

No book is written alone. This one is the fruit of many voices, hands, and hearts.

I sincerely thank my ancestors—those who resisted, prayed, and taught us to walk with dignity in a broken world. Their wisdom and struggle live on in every page.

To the Haitian people, whose courage and creativity defy despair, this book is for you. You have taught me that democracy is not a theory but a beat, a breath, a refusal to disappear.

I am grateful to my professor of Latin American politics at Syracuse University, Katrina Burgess, who suggested that I write a proposal about democracy in Haiti in partial fulfillment of the requirements for the master of arts in international relations degree program. My deepest thanks to all my instructors, especially my professor of international human rights, Donna E. Arzt, who required that her students pick an original topic for her law class. When I emailed her my topic, "Fostering Democracy and Human Rights in Haiti: An Examination of Haitian Democracy," she gave me valuable suggestions and said it was a good topic for my master's degree thesis. After completing the study, she encouraged me to work on it for publication, so I wrote Politics, Gangs, and Vodou: Haiti's Struggle for Democracy and Human Rights. I used the ideas I developed about the Haitian press for my thesis for my bachelor's of science degree in mass communications from the State University of Haiti to expand the book. Therefore, I also give deepest thanks to professors Frank L. Gilles, who was the committee chair, and Lucien Jean-Bernard and Armary Noël, the committee members who encouraged and gave me the strength to carry my study on the Haitian press forward to open the door for me to advance my education in the United States.

I am grateful to the researchers, historians, journalists, and activists whose work I have drawn upon, especially those who continue to tell the truth at great personal cost. May your bravery never go unnoticed. I am also grateful to my editors for their valuable suggestions.

To my family, relatives, and friends, especially my nephew Harry Jazon Jr., who did a lot of research for me; thanks for your encouragement, which gave me the strength to carry this book forward.

And finally, to the divine presence that surrounds and sustains: thank you for the silence in which this book was born and the fire in which it was forged.

Yvon Milien was born in Port-au-Prince, Haiti, and received a bachelor's of science in civil engineering from the Institut Supérieur Technique d'Haïti. He earned a bachelor's of science in mass communications from the State University of Haiti, where he wrote a thesis titled *"Position de la Presse dans la Vie Sociale Haitienne: Recherches sur l'Orientation que Donne le Contenu Educatif de la Presse pour Equilibrer la Vie Sociale"* ("The Press's Position in Haitian Social Life: A Study of the Orientation of the Content of the Media to Sustain Haitian Political and Social Life") for the Department of Human Sciences.

In 1997, he obtained a master's degree in sociology from Brigham Young University, where he authored a thesis titled "Haitian Mormon Converts Dwelling in New York City: A Cross-Cultural Perspective in Understanding, Interpreting, and Experiencing the Mormon Subculture."

In 2000, Milien obtained master's degrees in international relations and public administration from Syracuse University, where he authored a thesis titled "Fostering Democracy and Human Rights in Haiti: An Examination of Haitian Democracy."

In 2004, he earned a master's degree in education from the City University of New York, where he authored a thesis titled "The Effectiveness of Graphic Organizers and Baxendell's Guiding Principles for Instructional Practices with Special-Needs Students."